CO-CCA-922

Foreign Exchange Exposure in Emerging Markets

Foreign Exchange Exposure in Emerging Markets

How Companies Can Minimize It

Gastón Fornés

University of Bristol (UK) and ESIC Business and Marketing School (Spain)

First published 2009 by
PALGRAVE MACMILLAN

Palgrave Macmillan in the UK is an imprint of Macmillan Publishers Limited, registered in England, company number 785998, of Houndmills, Basingstoke, Hampshire RG21 6XS.

Palgrave Macmillan in the US is a division of St Martin's Press LLC, 175 Fifth Avenue, New York, NY 10010.

Palgrave Macmillan is the global academic imprint of the above companies and has companies and representatives throughout the world.

Palgrave® and Macmillan® are registered trademarks in the United States, the United Kingdom, Europe and other countries.

ISBN-13: 978–0–230–20260–3 hardback
ISBN-10: 0–230–20260–8 hardback

This book is printed on paper suitable for recycling and made from fully managed and sustained forest sources. Logging, pulping and manufacturing processes are expected to conform to the environmental regulations of the country of origin.

A catalogue record for this book is available from the British Library.

Library of Congress Cataloging-in-Publication Data
Gastón, Fornés, 1971–
Foreign exchange exposure in emerging markets : how companies can minimize it / Gastón Fornés.
p. cm.
Includes bibliographical references and index.
ISBN 978-0-230-20260-3
1. Foreign exchange rates–Developing countries. 2. Developing countries–Economic conditions. 3. Corporations, European–Finance. I. Title.
HG3877.F67 2008
332.4'56091724–dc22 2008020804

10 9 8 7 6 5 4 3 2 1
18 17 16 15 14 13 12 11 10 09

Printed and bound in Great Britain by
Antony Rowe Ltd, Chippenham and Eastbourne

To Claudia

To my parents

Contents

List of Figures

List of Tables

List of Boxes

Acknowledgements

First, I would like to thank the organizations that financially supported this project, the AlBan Programme from the European Union (high level scholarships for Latin America, identification number E03D21204AR), the University of Bath's School of Management, and ESIC Business and Marketing School. I also want to thank the Department of Politics at the University of Bristol for giving me the flexibility to work on this research.

Second, I would like to express my gratitude to the persons and organizations that, in different ways, helped me during this process: the University of Bath (especially the Research Support Unit), the School of Management, the Universidad del Desarrollo in Chile, the Consejo Empresario Mendocino, the IAE, the Alta Direccion Escuela de Negocios in Argentina, and all the persons and companies that took part in the survey.

Third, I am pleased to acknowledge the support received from the Euro-Latin American Centre at the Instituto de Empresa Business School in Spain; especially from its Director, Prof. G. Cardoza. His cooperation and guidance during the data collection stage in Madrid, along with the comments and engaging discussions when producing the paper presented at the EIBA conference in Oslo, created a place for deep reflections over the course of the last two years.

Fourth, I would like to thank Prof. Rafael Ortega and Prof. Segundo Huarte from ESIC; their support during the latest stages of this work is really appreciated.

Finally, and most importantly, I would like to thank Dr Alan Butt-Philip; without him this work would not have been possible. Alan, thank you very much, I am endlessly grateful.

Gastón Fornés

1
Introduction

> To my knowledge no model projecting movements in exchange rates is superior to tossing a coin.
>
> Alan Greenspan[1]

1.1 Context and motivation

This quote from Alan Greenspan highlights just how difficult it is for companies operating with different currencies to project the variations in the exchange rate. Dealing with different currencies began to be an issue for companies and governments principally after the end of the Bretton Woods system in 1973 and has been the reason behind many important political and economic agreements – one prime example being the European Union's (EU) Economic and Monetary Union (EMU) and the launch of the euro. The increase in international trade and investments following the end of the Second World War encouraged companies find new ways to deal with this issue, especially after 1973. Financial tools were developed to hedge currencies and strategies and organizational forms were proposed to protect the firm's value against unanticipated variations in the exchange rate.

Nevertheless, fluctuations in the exchange rate continued to be a major issue for companies and a new challenge appeared when what are now known as the emerging countries increased their share of international trade and became recipients of large amounts of foreign investment. The rise of the Latin American economies (principally Argentina, Brazil, Chile and Mexico), some Asian Pacific countries, and East European states following the dissolution of the Soviet Union in the 1990s, along with the economic emergence of China, India, and Russia in the first few years of the twenty-first century, are good examples of the increasing importance of these markets in the global economy. In this context, the economic integration among these emerging regions and industrialized countries has continued growing through more trade and investments as well as through the signing of Free Trade Agreements (FTAs) and the accession of many of these countries to the World Trade Organization (WTO).

As a consequence of this upward trend in investments and trade, for example, Western European companies became the largest investors in some of these regions, principally Latin America and Eastern Europe, and have also established significant positions in other emerging countries, such as India and Russia. But these positions did not prevent European firms from suffering as a result of the volatility in the price of these countries' currencies, especially during the economic and financial crises that occurred in Mexico (1994), Russia (1997), the Asia Pacific region (1997), Brazil (1999), Turkey (1999) and Argentina (2001) and their contagious effect on neighbouring countries.

The main sources of motivation for this work were the challenges faced by companies during currency crises in emerging markets. Many academic works have studied the foreign exchange (FX) exposure of companies from Triad countries operating in Triad countries; however, only a few were found researching this phenomenon for subsidiaries in emerging countries. On the other hand, during the years when the majority of this work was being carried out, important events occurred in relation to currencies in the global economy. For example, the consolidation of the euro, along with the loss of around 30 per cent of the value of the US dollar (against the European currency), provided specialized publications and companies with room for discussion about the different alternatives to deal with this new environment. The novelty in these discussions came from the inclusion of a debate on the value of an emerging country's currency, the Chinese renminbi.[2] The latter also shows the increasing importance of emerging markets in the international economy and therefore provided an extra source of motivation for this work.

Within the framework of these motivations, the question driving the efforts during this research was: what can companies do to protect the value of their investments in emerging markets against fluctuations in the exchange rate in a context of increasing economic integration? As mentioned earlier, the review of the literature showed that most of the research carried out in this field was focused on industrialized countries. In addition, most of them took a macro perspective (that is, one that studies industries or economic sectors). Only in recent years have the majority of the studies at the company level been published, but there has still been an overwhelming focus on the situation in developed or OECD countries.

Most of these works have concluded that because of the long-term nature of economic exposure (which is the name given to the most important, exposure resulting from the variations in the exchange rate), along with the problems encountered in trying to assess its effects accurately, their potential effects are difficult to hedge using the traditional techniques available in financial markets. Another conclusion presented by the literature is that companies should use their knowledge, assets, and skills in marketing, operations management, and finance in order to deal with this risk, and also that it must be included in the strategic planning of these areas.

It is for these reasons that the starting point of this work, and therefore its main proposition, is that a holistic approach (involving the functional areas mentioned before) to hedging against variations in the exchange rate is expected to contribute to a reduction of the impacts that these variations have in the performance of companies with foreign investments in emerging markets. The result of more than three years of work, and coinciding with the end of this project, this holistic approach has been recognised as one of the areas of future joint research between International Business and Finance, highlighting the importance of the effects of foreign exchange risk management on 'the MNE's [multinational enterprises] logistics, supply chain management, financial accounting, AIS, HR/OB, business law, and marketing functions' (Butler, 2006). Therefore, the first objective of this work is to study the movements in the exchange rate's impact on companies operating in emerging markets from a wider approach than has been taken by previous studies.

In addition, in order to answer the main question behind this research (presented in a previous paragraph), this work has also aimed to develop a tool to enable companies to improve the effectiveness of their hedging activities in emerging markets. This tool has been based on previous works on industrialized countries and has benefited from some adaptations to the emerging countries' environment based upon the data collected from companies operating in these markets. In this context, the second objective of this work is to attempt to develop a tool that helps companies to improve the effectiveness of their hedging activities in emerging markets.

Taken as a whole, the fact that foreign investments in emerging markets have continued growing with the emergence of the so-called 'BRIC' countries (that is, Brazil, Russia, India, and China), along with the recent recognition of the holistic approach taken, give current relevance to the topic under study. Furthermore, the development of a tool tailored to the companies' hedging needs is expected to have an impact on the management and performance of multinational corporations (MNCs) operating in emerging markets.

1.2 Structure

This introductory chapter is followed by a chapter on the global economy and emerging markets which aims to frame the context and also to provide some background for the analysis that forms the core of the book. This second chapter includes sections on the relative position of emerging markets in the global economy, and on the foreign investment trends in these markets, along with the main research perspectives used to analyse emerging markets.

Chapter 3 presents a review of the current literature. It begins with the main conceptual frameworks on the internationalization of companies, and then continues with the literature on foreign exchange exposure and its effects on firms' value from four different perspectives: finance, marketing, operations management, and strategic planning. The main approaches to assess the impact of exchange rate fluctuations are also included.

Chapter 4 introduces both the conceptual framework and the objectives of this work. It presents different perspectives – from finance, from marketing, from operations management, and from strategic planning. The main framework is constructed through the use of these four perspectives. The chapter concludes by giving an outline of the objectives and research propositions.

Chapter 5 shows how the analysis was carried out using the framework described in Appendix 1 at the end of the volume. It presents a detailed explanation of each part of the research process, starting from the definition of the research philosophy and design employed, continuing with the sample, the collection of data, and the analysis of both the quantitative and qualitative data. It finishes by showing how the quantitative and qualitative analyses were treated.

Chapter 6 is one of the most important in the book because it shows how the data were obtained, treated, and analysed. The chapter contains a section describing the results of the quantitative analysis, which is followed by a section including the results of the qualitative analysis. Finally, it shows how these two analyses complement, confirm, and corroborate each other in the "mixed methods" section.

Chapter 7 presents the most important part of this work – the development of a tool to minimize the foreign exchange exposure of companies operating in emerging markets. It is divided into two main sections – conclusions and recommendations. The first section analyses the findings (from Chapter 6) in the context of the current literature, with a special focus on the three research streams presented in Chapter 2: institutions theory, transaction costs economics, and the resource-based view of the firm. The second (and final) section offers the development of a tool and explains how companies can benefit from this research.

Finally, Chapter 8 gives an application of the model, which was undertaken for a group of companies operating in seven emerging markets. Throughout the chapter, the hedging activities of these companies are analysed and conclusions are obtained using the framework described in the previous chapters.

2
The Global Economy and the Emerging Markets

2.1 Introduction

This chapter will introduce the macro framework used in this study. In order to do this, it contains a review of the literature on international trade, on foreign investments, on emerging markets' characteristics, and, finally, on how they are related to exchange rate risk.

2.2 International trade

> The basis of international trade is exchange and specialization. International differences in the availability of raw materials and other factors of production lead to international differences in production costs and goods prices. Through international exchange, countries supply the world economy with the commodities that they produce relatively cheaply and demand from the world economy the goods made relatively cheaply elsewhere. (Begg et al., 2000)

Over the course of the past 2,000 years, international trade has played an important role in the attempts of national economies to supply their citizens with those raw materials and products they cannot produce at a competitive price, exchanging them for their surplus domestic products or raw materials. The first formal records of this kind of trade come from the Roman Empire and its *Pax Romana*. Since that time, international trade has been an ever-present and widespread phenomenon. However, among other turbulent political moments in history, there was one particular period when international trade almost ground to a halt. This period started at the beginning of the twentieth century with the outbreak of the First World War, continued through the Great Depression of the 1930s, and continued through the Second World War. According to Begg et al. (2000), 'It was not until the 1960s that world trade again reached its level of 1928'. From this time, world trade has assumed an increasing importance in the global community. In fact, in the past 20 years alone, the volume of international trade has expanded from US$200 billion to US$11,783 billion (WTO, 2007).

The origins of international trade theories can be traced back to the eighteenth century. By this time, gold was the world currency and governments attempted to enhance the country's economic well-being by stimulating exports and discouraging imports, accumulating gold as a consequence of the positive trade balance. This theory is called Mercantilism (Mitchell, 1967).

Another explanation of the reasons why nations trade with one another can be found in theories that are based on the idea of specialization. First, the theory of absolute advantage (Smith & Sutherland, 1993) states that countries can improve their economic well-being by specializing in the production of those goods in which they are most efficient. This simple model implies that if one nation has an absolute advantage when producing a good, this nation has the potential to benefit from trade. As a consequence, the higher the specialization in this good, the higher the potential gains in national well-being. However, this theory does not address the exchange ratio between products or how to distribute the benefits from trade between the countries. In addition, Rugman et al. (2006) recognised that the 'competitive market does not evenly distribute the gains from trade within one country'.

Secondly, the theory of comparative advantage presented in 1817 by David Ricardo (2002) states that countries should focus on the production of those products in which they have the greatest relative advantage. The principle here is that benefits from trade exist when the relative price ratios of two products are different in the international markets, compared with a situation in which international trade does not exist. This theory arrives at similar conclusions to the previous one; however, in addition it showed that countries can together benefit from free trade, even if one of them has an advantage in more than one product, as aggregate efficiency and consumption grow. However, the theory of comparative advantage still does not solve the dilemma of the distribution of gains between countries or how the benefits from trade would be shared within the country.

A third theory, labelled the factor endowment theory, was developed by Heckscher and Ohlin (1933). This theory states that countries should produce and export those goods that require a large amount of the production factors of which they have an abundant supply; and that they should import the products whose production requires the use of those factors they do not possess in great amounts. This theory expands the previous one of comparative advantages by including the cost of production of factors and also the level of endowment. However, it shows some weaknesses when including some regulations in the analysis, such as minimum wages in a country with a relatively large labour force, or in its application to some countries where the result is the contrary, as in the case of the US. The latter is known as the Leontief paradox (1954), which includes the quality of labour as a variable in addition to simply the number of working hours.

In one of the next developments, Vernon (1966) advanced the international product life cycle theory. This theory considers the various stages of a product's life cycle and is based upon the assumptions that technology plays a crucial role in creating and developing new products, and that both the size and structure of the market are important in defining patterns of trade. The theory divides the life cycle of a product into three different stages: new, maturing, and standardized. During the new stage, sales are in the home country, the price is inelastic, profits are higher, and consumers are willing to pay a premium for this new product. Then, during the maturing stage, the product is increasingly exported and competitors are trying to develop substitutes. Finally, in the third, standardized stage, the technology that was original and novel in the new stage is now easily available and production tends to be concentrated in low-cost locations. By analysing these stages from the point of view of different countries, it would be possible to see how trade may take place among all of them (original producer, competitor, exporter, importer, low-cost, and so on).

International trade is also affected by barriers. Generally, these barriers are set by the governments to encourage local production or to discourage foreign firms from operating in their domestic markets. Governments may also seek to help local firms with subsidies. Rugman et al. (2006) said that other common reasons include to:

- 'protect local jobs by shielding home-country business from foreign competition,
- encourage local production to replace imports,
- protect infant industries that are just getting started,
- reduce reliance on foreign suppliers,
- encourage local and foreign direct investments,
- reduce balance of payments problems,
- promote export activity,
- prevent foreign firms from dumping (selling goods below cost in order to achieve market share),
- promote political objectives such as refusing to trade with countries that practice apartheid or deny civil liberties to their citizens'.

Different barriers are used to deter the flow of goods and services by governments. Barriers can be based on price – for example, when a tariff is added to the price of goods, making it more expensive for domestic consumers. Barriers can also be set on quantity; in this case, they restrict the amount of units to be imported through the application of quotas. A third type of barrier is the fixation of the price or quantity to influence the international price of the goods, a practice called 'cartel'. Fourthly, financial restrictions, such as exchange controls, are also usually employed by governments as trade barriers. Fifthly, countries may establish controls to foreign investments in the form of minority ownerships, the limitation of profit remittance, or prohibiting the payments of royalties to the parent company. Table 2.1 shows a list of the most commonly found non-tariff barriers.

Table 2.2 presents the world's leading importers and exporters in 2006. In this table, it is important to highlight that around 70 per cent of world trade is concentrated in only ten countries (or regions, in the case of the EU).

2.3 The global economy

The rise in international trade described in the previous section and the cross-border flows of capital are the most notable expressions of what is now termed the global economy (Brakman et al., 2006).

Table 2.1 Common non-tariff barriers to trade

Specific limitation	Customs administrative rules	Government participation	Import charges
Quotas (including voluntary)	Valuation systems	Procurement policies	Import deposits
Import licences	Anti-dumping rules	Export subsidies and incentives	Supplementary duties
Supplementary incentives	Packaging, labelling, and marketing standards	Countervailing duties	Import credits
Minimum import limits	Documentation needed	Domestic assistance programmes	Variable levies
Sectoral bilateral agreements	Fees	Trade-diverting	Border levies
Embargoes	Disparities in quality and testing standards		
Orderly marketing agreements	Tariff classifications		

Source: Rugman et al. (2006).

Although there is a debate on the exact meaning of 'global' it is possible to analyse its main features using the following five perspectives:

a. *Cultural*: international trade brings products from one country to the rest of the world. These products carry a cultural attachment and disseminate the country of origin's culture to the consumers in the host nation; the best examples of this are the movies produced in Hollywood. The Internet is also playing a key role in the globalization of culture.
b. *Economic*: national domestic markets have declined in importance and now international markets are the companies' main focus. This change has taken place not only in final goods, but also in intermediate goods or the procurement of production factors such as labour and capital. This phenomenon has created what Neary (2003) described as an 'increased interdependence of national economies, and the trend towards greater integration of goods, labour, and capital markets'.

Table 2.2 Leading importers and exporters in world merchandise trade (excluding intra-EU trade) 2006 (billions of US dollars and %)

Rank	Exporters	Value	Share	Annual % var.	Rank	Importers	Value	Share	Annual % var.
1	Extra-EU (25) exports	1481.7	16.4	11	1	United States	1919.4	20.5	11
2	United States	1038.3	11.5	15	2	Extra-EU (25) imports	1697.8	18.1	15
3	China	968.9	10.7	27	3	China	791.5	8.5	20
4	Japan	649.9	7.2	9	4	Japan	579.6	6.2	13
5	Canada	389.5	4.3	8	5	Canada	357.7	3.8	11
6	Korea, Republic of	325.5	3.6	14	6	Hong Kong, China	335.8	3.6	12
7	Hong Kong, China	322.7	3.6	10	7	Korea, Republic of	309.4	3.3	18
8	Russian Federation	304.5	3.4	25	8	Mexico	268.2	2.9	15
9	Singapore	271.8	3.0	18	9	Singapore	238.7	2.5	19
10	Mexico	250.4	2.8	17	10	Taipei, Chinese	203.0	2.2	11
	Sub total	**6003**	**66.5**			**Sub total**	**6701**	**71.6**	
11	Taipei, Chinese	223.8	2.5	13	11	India	174.8	1.9	26
12	Saudi Arabia	209.5	2.3	16	12	Russian Federation[1]	163.9	1.8	31
13	Malaysia	160.7	1.8	14	13	Switzerland	141.4	1.5	12
14	Switzerland	147.5	1.6	13	14	Australia	139.3	1.5	11
15	United Arab Emirates	139.4	1.5	19	15	Turkey	138.3	1.5	18
16	Brazil	137.5	1.5	16	16	Malaysia	131.2	1.4	14
17	Thailand	130.8	1.4	19	17	Thailand	128.6	1.4	9
18	Australia	123.3	1.4	16	18	United Arab Emirates	97.8	1.0	15
19	Norway	121.5	1.3	17	19	Brazil	95.9	1.0	24
20	India	120.3	1.3	21	20	Indonesia	80.3	0.9	6
21	Indonesia	103.5	1.1	19	21	South Africa[2]	77.3	0.8	24
22	Turkey	85.5	0.9	16	22	Saudi Arabia	66.3	0.7	12
23	Iran, Islamic Rep. of[2]	73.7	0.8	31	23	Norway	64.1	0.7	15

(Continued)

Table 2.2 Continued

Rank	Exporters	Value	Share	Annual % var.	Rank	Importers	Value	Share	Annual % var.
24	Bolivarian Rep. of Venezuela	65.2	0.7	18	24	Philippines[1]	51.5	0.6	9
25	South Africa	58.4	0.6	13	25	Romania	51.1	0.5	26
26	Chile	58.1	0.6	41	26	Iran, Islamic Rep. of[2]	51.1	0.5	34
27	Kuwait	55.7	0.6	24	27	Israel[2]	50.0	0.5	6
28	Algeria	54.6	0.6	19	28	Ukraine	45.0	0.5	25
29	Nigeria[2]	52.0	0.6	23	29	Viet Nam	44.4	0.5	20
30	Philippines	47.0	0.5	14	30	Chile	38.4	0.4	17
31	Argentina	46.6	0.5	15	31	Argentina	34.2	0.4	19
32	Israel	46.4	0.5	9	32	Bolivarian Rep. of Venezuela	33.6	0.4	40
33	Kazakhstan	40.5	0.4	45	33	Pakistan	29.8	0.3	18
34	Viet Nam	39.6	0.4	22	34	Iraq[2]	27.9	0.3	19
35	Libyan Arab Jamahiriya[2]	39.5	0.4	28	35	New Zealand	26.4	0.3	1
36	Ukraine	38.4	0.4	12	36	Colombia	26.0	0.3	23
37	Angola[2]	35.0	0.4	45	37	Kazakhstan	25.0	0.3	44
38	Qatar	34.1	0.4	32	38	Morocco	23.6	0.3	13
39	Romania	32.3	0.4	17	39	Bulgaria	23.1	0.2	27
40	Iraq[2]	29.6	0.3	25	40	Belarus	22.3	0.2	34

[1] Imports are valued f.o.b.
[2] Secretariat estimates.
Source: WTO (2007).

c. *Geographical*: distance has diminished its importance; this is mainly the consequence of the reduced time and cost of travel along with the possibility of rapid exchanges of information.
d. *Institutional*: the creation of global institutions and the pursuit of strategies influenced by global trends. The World Trade Organization (WTO) is an example of the former, whereas companies taking similar policies due to competitive and regulatory pressures are an example of the latter.
e. *Political*: the relation between the nation-state and the market has changed over the last 50 years, from cooperation after the Second World War to the firms' distinctive role in the allocation of resources over the last 15 years (Brakman et al., 2006; McDonald & Burton, 2002).

2.4 The global economy and the Triad

International trade is concentrated within ten countries/regions, as is shown in Table 2.2. The core of these ten countries/regions is dominated by what is known as the Triad, formed by the EU-15, the US, and Japan. In recent years, the Triad has expanded its area of influence to neighbouring countries in the form of: (i) regional agreements, such as in the case of the North American Free Trade Agreement (NAFTA) with Mexico, Canada, and the US; (ii) further integration, such as the EU's expansions in 2004 and 2007; or (iii) the emergence of trading countries in East Asia, such as South Korea, Singapore, Hong Kong, Taipei, and China. The trade between these areas can be seen in Table 2.3. It is possible to see from this table the difference between the trade within these regions and their interregional trade in comparison with the rest of the world.

The predominance of the Triad in international trade is expected to continue. However, it is also expected that other countries will continue increasing their presence on the world trade stage. This expectation is supported by the growth of the participation of emerging markets in world trade, a case in point being the emergence of China over the last ten years. This growth can be seen by comparing the data in Table 2.4, trade patterns in 1996, and the figures presented in Table 2.2, which shows the amounts traded in 2006.

Table 2.3 Intra- and inter-regional merchandise trade, 2006 (billions of US dollars)

	Destination							
Origin	**North America**	**South Central America**	**Europe**	**CIS**	**Africa**	**Middle East**	**Asia**	**World**
North America	**905**	107	**279**	8	22	42	**314**	1,678
South and Central America	135	111	86	6	11	8	62	430
Europe	**430**	67	**3,651**	142	120	129	**366**	4,963
CIS	24	8	246	80	6	13	46	426
Africa	80	11	148	1	33	6	73	363
Middle East	72	4	103	3	21	72	340	645
Asia	**708**	69	**604**	50	70	111	**1,638**	3,278
World	2,355	378	5,118	290	283	381	2,839	11,783

Source: WTO (2007).

Table 2.4 Trade patterns, 1996

% of world trade from	**Industrial Countries**	**Less Developed Countries**
Industrial Countries	50%	18%
Less Developed Countries	18%	14%
% of world income	80%	20%

Source: World Bank (1996).

2.5 The global economy and trade agreements

Another piece of evidence can be found in the growth of trade agreements between developing countries and industrial economies: in the 1990s, the expansion in the number of FTAs can be attributed principally to the collapse of the COMECON, the preferential arrangement involving the old Soviet Union and Eastern European countries, as well as the alignment of the Central and Eastern European countries to the European Union. For example, of the more than 120 new regional trade agreements (RTAs) in force since 1990, approximately one-third were signed between transition economies.

In addition, between 30 and 40 per cent of all RTAs currently in force (including those not notified to the WTO) involved agreements among developing countries. There is also some evidence that FTAs between developed and developing countries have increased over the years; since 2000, developing countries have participated in 50 per cent of the new FTAs. In this respect, the EU has played an important role through a series of agreements with countries such as Turkey, Mexico, South Africa, and Chile (WTO, 2003). Table 2.5 shows a summary of notified RTAs in goods by the date of entry into force and type of partners.[1]

In addition, recent years have seen a rise in cross-regional RTAs and also the involvement of more countries in this kind of arrangement. For instance, around one-third of the FTAs negotiated since 2002 are among countries that belong to different geographical areas and, at the same time, countries that have traditionally remained outside regional agreements are now negotiating and joining RTAs. A key example of the latter is Japan, which signed an FTA with Singapore and has been negotiating with Canada, Chile, Mexico and the Philippines. FTAs are also taking different forms; many are going beyond the removal of tariff barriers and quotas and are including the removal or reduction of non-tariff barriers.

In this context, 43 per cent of world merchandise trade in 2003 occurred under the umbrella of preferential trade arrangements, a proportion that is increasing as more and more RTAs are negotiated. In fact, it is estimated that, by the end of 2006, more than 50 per cent of world merchandise trade took place within some kind of preferential agreement. This situation can be seen in Table 2.6, which shows preferential trade share of intra-RTAs.[2]

2.6 Emerging markets in the global economy

Arnold and Quelch (1998) stated that

> emerging markets constitute the major growth opportunity in the evolving world economic order. Their potential has already effected a shift in multinational companies (MNCs), which now customarily highlight investments in emerging markets when

Table 2.5 Regional trade agreements in goods by the date of entry into force and type of partners (as of January 2003)

	Developed Developed	Developed Developing	Developed Transition	Developing Developing	Developing Transition	Transition Transition	Total
1958–1964	2	0	0	1	0	0	**3**
1965–1969	0	0	0	0	1	0	**1**
1970–1974	5	3	0	2	0	0	**10**
1975–1979	0	5	0	1	0	0	**6**
1980–1984	2	1	0	1	0	0	**4**
1985–1989	1	1	0	2	0	0	**4**
1990–1994	3	3	12	5	0	6	**29**
1995–1999	3	7	10	4	12	28	**64**
2000–2002	0	11	4	5	4	6	**30**
Total	**16**	**31**	**26**	**21**	**17**	**40**	**151**

Source: WTO (2003).

Table 2.6 Preferential trade share of intra-RTAs trade in merchandise imports of major regions, 2000 and 2005 (%)

	2000	2005
Western Europe	64.7	67.0
Transition Economies	61.6	61.6
North America (incl. Mexico)	41.4	51.6
Africa	37.2	43.6
Middle East	19.2	38.1
Latin America (excl. Mexico)	18.3	63.6
Asia	5.6	16.2
World	**43.2**	**51.2**

Source: WTO (2003).

communicating with shareholders . . . These investments are widely interpreted as heralds of a major restructuring of the global economy.

Arnold and Quelch also affirmed that

the new perception of these countries as markets explains the surge of interest. The phrase 'emerging markets' (EMs) is being adopted in place of the previous lexicon of 'less developed countries', newly industrializing countries, or even Third World countries, which emphasized the countries' sources of cheap raw materials and labour rather than their markets. The EMs' new attractiveness is partly explained by their emergence and a number of economic liberalization measures prompted, in some cases, by the demise of communist governments. However, it is also a function of global factors, notably the competition among MNCs in maturing markets in the developed economies.

These markets seem to present a good opportunity to commercialize what Levitt (1983) has called globally standardized products and, therefore, for MNCs to capitalize the R&D already invested in developed countries. In addition, these regions seem to have sufficient critical size to make it worthwhile developing new products. In addition, as Brewer and Young (1998) pointed out, the dynamic effect of liberalization of these countries suggests that per capita income growth will further increase the market potential, and at the same time, the possibilities to generate returns to scale. Rugman and Hodgetts (2003) also mentioned that many MNCs have decided whether or not to make investments in emerging markets on the basis of being closer to the market as a means of improving customer service, as well as to tailor production to local market needs. Other reasons usually mentioned for operating in emerging markets are incentives offered by the countries, as well as low-cost assets, labour, or energy.

In this context, Rugman et al. (2006) stated that emerging markets are:

- 'growing in importance for international managers for both market-seeking investments and resource-seeking investments,
- strongly government-controlled, in that government agencies play a central role in negotiating with foreign investors and deciding the local rules of the game,
- less predictable and riskier than triad markets, which investors often underestimate in their pursuit of the high level of rewards on offer, and
- the source of new competitors, as local firms move up the value chain, becoming more sophisticated and more international'.

These authors also stated that companies from the Triad and from emerging markets are increasingly competing in each other's markets. The reasons they give for this can be seen in the matrix presented in Figure 2.1.

2.7 Foreign investments in emerging markets[3]

In addition, the participation of emerging markets in the global economy can also be seen in the amount of foreign investments in these regions. Foreign direct investment (FDI), as described by Kobrin (1977), implies that a foreign investor acquires control of a new or existing local operation. In this context, control represents the managerial sense of decision-making power. Although there is no consensus on the stake needed to exercise this control, definitions from most countries and from major international institutions mention a range of between 10 and 25 per cent (Alfaro & Clavell, 2002).

	Triad firms in non-Triad regions	Non-Triad firms in Triad regions
Market-seeking	Growing disposable and growing markets; potential future lead markets	Large, mature markets; large disposable incomes; home-base of many client companies and flagship firms
Resource-seeking	Cheaper (sometimes better) labour, land, resources, materials, and/or suppliers	Specific technological expertise and managerial capabilities: specialist suppliers, capital

Figure 2.1 A summary of reasons why companies from the Triad and from emerging markets invest in each others' home regions
Source: Rugman et al. (2006).

In addition, Fernandez-Arias and Hausmann (2000) said that managerial control could also entail investments with returns expected in longer periods. These control and long-term investments contrast with what is known as portfolio investments, which mean the purchase of local firm's securities or bonds without exercising control (Alfaro & Clavell, 2002). Kobrin (1977) also observed that FDI gives host countries the opportunity to receive a flow of resources such as managerial skills, technology, and marketing knowledge, accompanied (or not) by capital transfers.

Table 2.7 presents the capital inflows between 1978 and 1995. This table also shows the inflows to less developed countries (LDCs) by type. As can be seen from the table, in these years the composition of capital inflows shifted from bank loans towards FDI and portfolio investment. Furthermore, the FDI proportion increased more than three times during the period. Hence, LDCs are not only gaining

Table 2.7 Capital inflows by type, 1978–1995 (billions of US dollars and %)

	1978–81	1982–89	1990–95
Total Inflow (23 OECD and 61 LDCs)	442	578	1,050
Inflow to LDCs	68	24	135
% to LDCs	15.3	4.2	12.9
% FDI	13.2	53.7	39.8
% Portfolio Inv	3.1	9.0	38.5
% Loans	83.6	36.9	21.7

Source: Adapted from Bosworth & Collins (1999).

Table 2.8 FDI inflows (thousands of millions of US dollars)

	1998	1999	2000	2001	2002	2003	2004	2005	2006
World	4,168	4,939	5,810	6,211	6,789	8,185	9,571	10,048	11,999
LDCs	1,224	1,559	1,708	1,787	1,727	1,978	2,288	2,622	3,156
%	29.4	31.6	29.4	28.8	25.4	24.2	23.9	26.1	26.3

Source: UNCTAD (2007).

weight in world trade (as presented above), but they also increased their participation as recipients of FDI flows.

FDI inflows to emerging markets have also maintained an average participation of about 27.2 per cent between 1998 and 2006. To illustrate this, Table 2.8 shows FDI inflows by type of economy from 1998 to 2006.

In this context, Table 2.9 presents the top recipients of FDI among emerging markets up to 2006. As can be seen, only 12 countries account for more than 50 per cent of the total FDI stock to these markets. Moreover, six countries, three from Asia and three from Latin America, explain almost 40 per cent.

One other point to mention about FDI is its relative importance in emerging markets' economies. Table 2.8 showed that developed countries received the largest share of foreign investments; however, this nominal superiority is contrasted with FDI stocks as a percentage of GDP.

Figure 2.2 presents the relationship between FDI stocks and GDP as an average from 1995 to 2006 where four tiers can be identified: over

Table 2.9 Top FDI recipients among emerging markets (millions of US dollars)

	%	Total
China	9.3	292,559
Mercosur*	9.1	286,494
Mexico	7.2	228,601
Singapore	6.7	210,089
Russian Federation	6.3	197,682
Poland	3.3	103,616
Chile	2.6	80,732
Turkey	2.5	79,075
Czech Republic	2.5	77,460
South Africa	2.4	77,038
Republic of Korea	2.2	70,974
India	1.6	50,680
Total	**55.6**	**1,754,998**

*: Argentina + Brazil
Source: Author's calculations with data from UNCTAD (2007).

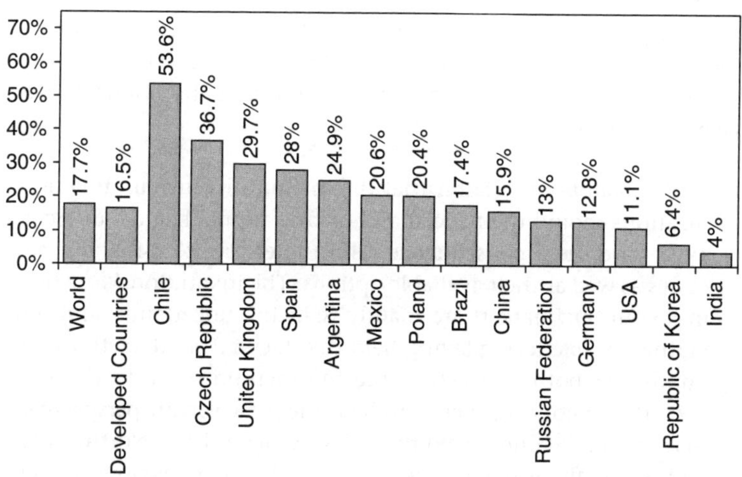

Figure 2.2 Inward FDI stocks as a percentage of GDP (average 1995–2006)
Source: UNCTAD (2007).

30 per cent of GDP, between 20 and 29.99 per cent, between 10 and 19.99 per cent, and from 0 to 9.99 per cent. As can be seen, in the first two tiers (20 to 29.99 per cent and over 30 per cent) mostly emerging markets are represented, with the exceptions of the UK and Spain. These figures suggest that MNCs have a significant participation in the economy of some emerging markets. Moreover, this fact, along with the 27 per cent of foreign investment headed to emerging markets, indicates that many emerging markets are an important part of the international strategy of most MNCs.

2.8 Emerging markets: main research perspectives

Most of the literature defines emerging markets as those that fulfil two characteristics: first, countries that are experiencing rapid economic development and, secondly, countries where their governments' policies are aimed at economic liberalization and the adoption of a free-market system (Arnold & Quelch, 1998). Within this definition, it is possible to find 64 emerging markets in the world: 51 developing countries in Asia, Latin America, Africa, and the Middle East identified by the International Financial Corporation, and 13 transition economies listed by the European Bank for Reconstruction and Development (Hoskisson et al., 2000).

Hoskisson et al. (2000) proposed the study of the environment of these emerging markets using three different perspectives: institutional theory, transaction costs economics, and the resource-based view of the firm:

a. *Institutional theory*: claims that the institutions surrounding organizations mould their social and organizational behaviour (Scott, 1995) and, as a consequence, affect their decision-making processes as well as their available options. The institutions' functions in a country [market] are mainly reducing uncertainty and providing a stable level playing field that facilitates interactions and diminishes both transaction and information costs. In this context, this theory has been studied under two main perspectives: first, from an economic point of view (Clague, 1997; North, 1990), and, secondly, using a sociological analysis (DiMaggio & Powell, 1983; Scott, 1995). In addition, the interaction between institutions and firms has also been studied (Harris et al., 1995) where

North (1990) said that institutions set the framework for social interaction and that organizations are bound to play within this structure.

Although it is generally claimed that there are only a limited number of theoretical and empirical studies that apply this theory to emerging markets, there are some interesting works in this area showing how organizations are affected by institutions. These studies share similar conclusions – that firms in emerging economies were influenced by existing institutional frameworks; however, in some cases this influence was negative (Child & Lu, 1996; Lau, 1998; Palmer, et al., 1993; Peng, 1997; Peng & Heath, 1996; Suhomlinova, 1999), whereas other works indicated a more positive influence (Jefferson & Rawski, 1995; Lee & Miller, 1996; Soulsby & Clark, 1996). This positive effect was seen mainly when it was found that institutions facilitate strategy-setting activities, giving the opportunity for organizations to react and take more active roles.

b. *Transaction costs economics*: 'studies the firm–environment interface through a contractual or exchange-based approach' (Williamson, 1975). In this context, 'the rational governance choice [for companies] requires a trade-off, at the margin, between the transaction costs associated with the market mode, a firm's need for control, and the governance costs of hierarchy' (Hoskisson et al., 2000).

This theory has been applied mainly to developed countries with strong legal regimes and binding social norms. Nevertheless, it is possible to find studies that use this theory in the context of emerging markets – and these tend to present conclusions in three main areas. First, transaction costs in emerging markets seem to be higher than those in developed economies principally when: (i) the price system does not give reliable information for the efficient allocation of resources and, as a consequence, the measurement of costs tends to be higher (Choi et al., 1999); and (ii) the government's discretion (rather than the rule of law) determines property rights and makes their enforcement more costly (La Porta et al., 1997). Secondly, hybrid governance structures, such as networks, seem to be an efficient alternative in emerging markets (dominating over both markets and hierarchies) as firms in these markets find it difficult to grow internally or through M&As due to the low enforcement of property rights and unstable political structures

(Peng & Heath, 1996). Thirdly, transaction costs appear to be the reason behind the high prevalence in emerging markets of: (i) unrelated diversification by large business groups, because of their underdeveloped capital and labour markets (Khanna & Palepu, 1997; Williamson, 1975); and (ii) countertrade, as it creates mutual commitments that can discourage opportunistic behaviour (Choi et al., 1999).

c. *Resource-based view of the firm*: the main focus of this theory is the assets that make each company different and represent the foundations of their competitive advantage (Penrose, 1959). These assets, in the form of resources and capabilities (usually intangible), can be assessed using four different criteria: value, rareness, inimitability, and substitutability (Barney, 1991). Companies should use these assets to generate rents, and to do that, firms need to be capable of developing institutional capital to optimize the use of these resources (Oliver, 1997). In this context, research using the resource-based view of the firm in emerging markets focuses on how companies use their value-creating assets in the specific context of these economies (Hoskisson et al., 2000).

In emerging markets, state Hoskisson et al. (2000), the development of these kinds of assets is difficult and, most of the time, implies the establishment of good relationships with the local government. For example, the authors continued, access to licences or distribution channels is often limited; in fact, they also recognised that the first mover advantage strategy can be undermined because of weak relations with the relevant government bodies. This could be one of the reasons why diversified business groups have grown in emerging markets, because they could obtain licences and other benefits as the result of their close links with the home government and, as a consequence, could protect their operations from domestic and international competitors. In other words, business groups 'may have developed capabilities for relationship-based management in their environment that substitute for the lack of institutional infrastructure' (Hoskisson et al., 2000) and base their competitive advantage on links with the authority. In conclusion, in emerging markets many competitive advantages seem to be 'based on network relationships and close business–government ties', and that, consequently, many firms have become 'effective monopolies in their home markets' (Hoskisson et al., 2000).

The pace of change and the rate of growth have not been uniform in the 64 identified emerging economies. For example, of the 13 transition economies in Eastern Europe, only a few have been successful in achieving the high standard of institutional development required to join the European Union. In addition, South East Asia, especially China, has been growing at a higher rate during the last ten years than other big countries such as Brazil or other neighbouring countries in Latin America. This situation calls for case-by-case analysis, considering the particular situation of each country (or regions in some cases) as the unit of study.

However, studies in emerging countries found some similar problems in the transformation of their economies. For example, in Eastern Europe the European Bank for Reconstruction and Development (1998) found that macroeconomic stability – the first key step for external economic assistance – has proved difficult to achieve, and that the creation of market institutions has been even harder. Hoskisson et al. (2000) complemented this opinion by stating that the political and economic crises in some of these countries along with weak institutional frameworks have helped to raise uncertainty and risks and, as a consequence, foreign companies may hesitate when deciding on investments. This situation seems to be the consequence of three main problems (some of them already mentioned above): (i) a weak definition of property rights, especially in the areas of exclusivity, transferability, and quality of title (Devlin et al., 1998); (ii) a weak legal framework allowing for opportunism, rent shifting, bribery, and corruption (Nelson et al., 1998); and (iii) the local government's (in)ability to enforce established legislation on property rights (Estrin & Wright, 1999). As a result, the development of sound institutions has been – and will continue to be – critical for attracting investments from foreign companies (Rondinelli, 1998).

Taken as a whole, the research studies mentioned above show that the particular environment in emerging countries has a significant effect upon the operations of companies, both international and domestic. This influence can be seen in three main areas: (i) institutional forces affect processes and decision-making; (ii) transaction costs are higher and have an impact on governance structures, on (unrelated) integration, and on the development of countertrade; and (iii) value-creating assets seem to be easier to develop/get when there are close links with local governments.

2.9 Transaction costs in emerging markets: the exchange rate risk

As shown in the previous sections, one of the criteria that often underlies various definitions of emerging markets 'is the system of market governance and, in particular, the extent and stability of a free market system' (Arnold & Quelch, 1998). In this context, Khanna and Palepu (2002) stated that 'an important measure of quality [of the market system] is the ease with which transactions can take place in any market and the cost associated with it. Emerging markets are those where markets are still emerging, so to speak. Hence, transaction costs are [likely to be] high'. This is mainly because the complex webs of institutions that permeate the developed economies are either absent or poorly developed in emerging countries. Therefore, 'even when countries embrace markets, they cannot create market institutions overnight'.

In this respect, the work of Khanna and Palepu (2002) analysed countries that have adopted free market reforms. They found that 'building all the institutional infrastructure for well-functioning markets is a slow and time consuming process'. Among their reasons, they mentioned: (i) that emerging markets require good political governance to develop institutions with thoughtful and supportive regulations, as well as even-handed and predictable enforcement; (ii) that these institutions need qualified persons with certain skills that are usually difficult to find in emerging economies; and (iii) that in the development of market institutions there is a mutual interdependence across the first two problems. Hoskisson et al. (2000) shared these findings. In conclusion, Khanna and Palepu suggested that 'many emerging markets are likely to suffer from significant institutional voids for a long time to come'. This conclusion also supports the results of their previous work: 'the mere deregulation of economies does not automatically lead to immediate reduction in transaction costs' (Khanna & Palepu, 2000).

Transaction costs are recurrent in the literature about the management of companies in emerging markets. For example, Guillén (2000) concluded that unrelated diversified business groups is an organizational form adopted by companies from emerging countries to compete in markets that fail. Likewise, Khanna and Palepu (2000) found that, in Chile, 'affiliates of the most extensively diversified business groups outperformed focused unaffiliated firms'.

In contrast, Hoskisson et al. (2000) stated that in a 'more advanced economy, diversification becomes less useful because external markets are more efficient'. These opinions support the fact that business groups may exist in the absence of a well-functioning market – that is, in a market with higher transaction costs. Del Sol and Kogan (2007) also recognised this difference by stating that companies' strategies in emerging markets require a period of transition until the conditions expected after economic reforms are achieved. It seems that studies in the field show that higher transaction costs make companies from emerging markets apply different strategies in their local market.

The exchange rate risk is part of these transaction costs and tends to affect emerging markets in a different way as their economic structure differs from that of the developed or industrialized countries. These differences are based mainly on the strategies that EMs have followed in an attempt to develop their economies (a more detailed analysis of the effects of the exchange rate risk at company level will be presented in the next chapter). A summary of these strategies can be seen in Box 1 (Begg et al., 2000).

The four strategies presented in Box 1 can affect the factors that influence what is known as the equilibrium exchange rate, both positive and negatively. These factors are described below (Madura, 1995) and shown in Figure 2.3:

- *Changes in relative inflation rates*: can affect international trade activity, and therefore the demand and supply of currencies;
- *Changes in relative interest rates*: can affect investment in foreign securities, and therefore the demand and supply of currencies;
- *Changes in relative income levels*: for example, an increase in income levels sometimes causes expectations of higher rates; so even though it can result in more imports, it may also indirectly attract more financial inflows (assuming interest rates increase), and vice versa;
- *Government controls*: can influence the equilibrium exchange rate in many ways, including the imposition of foreign exchange barriers, the imposition of foreign trade barriers, intervention (buying or selling currencies) in the foreign exchange markets, and the effect of macro variables such as inflation, interest rates, and income levels;

Box 1 A summary of the strategies pursued by emerging countries to develop their economies

a. *Development through trade in primary products*: in this case, emerging markets export agricultural goods and minerals to the rest of the world, using the revenue to obtain machinery and other manufactured imports. The problem with this strategy is the downward tendency of primary commodity prices. This trend can be attributed either to increased supply, such as improved productivity and output, or to reduced demand, as technical advances capable of substituting primary products. Furthermore, the prices of these products suffer from high volatility because both the supply and the demand are price-inelastic. For example, a long drought (supply side) will raise the prices of food as people will continue buying it (demand side). Consequently, these fluctuations in the price affect the export earnings and the GDP, especially of those LDCs with high concentration of exports in primary products.
b. *Development through industrialization*: two main sub-strategies can be identified. First, Import Substitution aims to develop domestic production of some kinds of goods under the protection of tariffs or import quotas. Despite its ambitious objectives, 'international trade theory suggests that this policy is likely to be wasteful' (Begg et al., 2000). Second, Export-led Growth pursues income growth through the production of manufactured goods to be exported. This strategy accounts for successful stories in the last three decades, especially for the countries of South East Asia (including China).
c. *Development through borrowing*: under this strategy, emerging economies can import capital goods through borrowing in world markets. Hence, they can finance an excess of imports over exports as well as supplement domestic investment.
d. *Development through structural adjustment*: this strategy involves the 'pursuit of supply-side policies aimed at increasing potential output by increasing efficiency' (Begg et al., 2000), with the intention to use the resources already available more efficiently.

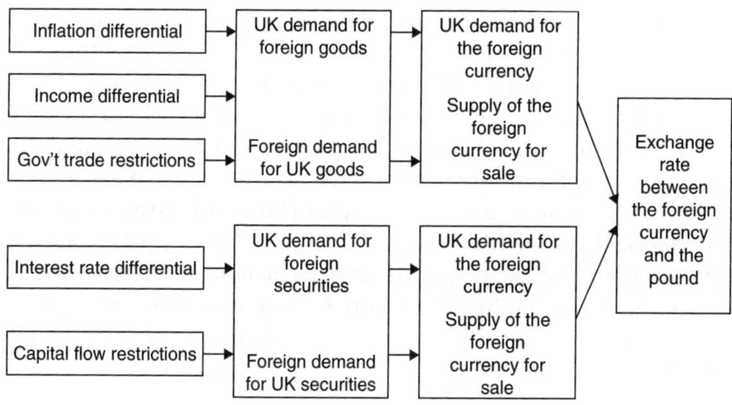

Figure 2.3 A summary of the factors affecting exchange rates, an example for the UK
Source: Adapted from Madura (1995).

- *Market expectations*: as a result of speculative behaviour, foreign exchange rates can be very volatile;
- *Interaction of factors*: trade-related factors and financial factors sometimes interact; for example, an increase in income levels is frequently expected to strengthen local currency because the favourable financial flows may overwhelm the unfavourable trade flows.

Figure 2.3 provides a summary of how trade-related and finance-related flows affect exchange rates. As can be seen, some factors may place upward pressure on the value of a foreign currency while others may place downward pressure on the currency's value (over a certain period of time). The sensitivity of an exchange rate to these factors is dependent upon the volume of international transactions between the two countries. The next sub-sections will present a short summary of how exchange rates are determined and how the international exchange system works, included in order to complement what has previously been explained.

2.9.1 Exchange rate: the basics

One national currency can be changed for another in an international market called the foreign exchange (forex) market. The nominal exchange rate is the price at which two currencies exchange, \$/£ for instance. Therefore, like any other products sold in markets, the price of a currency is determined by the demand for that currency relative to the supply. At any point in time, a currency should exhibit the price at which the demand for that currency is equal to the supply, and this represents the equilibrium exchange rate. Furthermore, in the context of international trade, it is also relevant to take into consideration the international competitiveness of a country. This competitiveness is gauged by the real exchange rate (RER), which 'measures the relative price of goods from different countries when measured in a common currency' (Begg et al., 2000), generally the US dollar. For example, the UK's real exchange rate in terms of US dollars can be expressed as:

$$\text{RER} = \left(\frac{\text{Price index of UK goods}}{\text{Price index of US goods}}\right) \times \left(\frac{\$}{£}\right) \tag{1}$$

From this equation emerges the purchasing power parity (PPP) exchange rate path, which is the 'path of the nominal exchange rate that would keep the RER constant over a given period' (Begg et al., 2000) and therefore compensate for the differences in inflation rates among countries and keep the RER at a constant level along with the level of competitiveness.

From the equation shown above, it is possible to see that there is only one RER in the long term, as in the long term the nominal exchange rate will keep the real competitiveness at a certain level. In other words, the nominal exchange rate will be adapting to differences in the domestic and foreign inflation rates to maintain constant the real competitiveness (in the absence of real shocks) as the nominal exchange rate will follow the PPP path (Begg et al., 2000).

2.9.2 The international exchange rate system: a short review

If countries are to trade, they must be able to exchange currencies. But at what rate should one currency be exchanged for another? To answer this question, nations have been adopting different monetary systems. In the 1870s, the introduction of the Gold Standard provided a framework for the international monetary system. This system 'was a monetary union based on fixed gold prices, convertible currencies, and complete gold backing for the money supply' (Begg et al., 2000) that was adopted until the outbreak of the First World War (McDonald & Burton, 2002). After the war, the Bank of England returned to the Gold Standard until 1931, when it abandoned the system. At the same time, during the 1920s and the 1930s, many countries decided to close their markets and to take protectionist measures trying to undercut each other through continual currency devaluations (Czinkota et al., 1996). In 1944, one year before the end of the Second World War, the Bretton Woods Agreement was signed. The main features of this agreement were the adjustable peg and the creation of both the International Monetary Fund (IMF) and the World Bank (WB). With this system, each country announced a par value for its currency against the dollar; in addition, each currency was convertible into dollars (rather than gold, as was the case in the Gold Standard era) (Begg et al., 2000). Following the agreement, every government was accountable for keeping the value of its currency between ranges of +/-1 per cent from the par value, and could ask for temporary loans from the IMF to adjust its balance of payments back towards equilibrium. In March 1973, the Bretton Woods system was abandoned, and most major currencies were allowed to float.

In 1979, the European Monetary System (EMS) encountered the same kind of adjustment problems that had confronted its predecessors, the Gold Standard and the Bretton Woods system – that is, divergent economic conditions among members could not be adjusted through domestic economic policies. The liberalization of capital markets in the 1980s led to an increase in the volume of international capital flows, and consequently the volatility of exchange rates increased – due in large part to the large growth in short-run capital flows. After these experiences, it seems that liquidity, confidence, and adjustment problems meant that no international monetary system capable of providing fixed exchange rates (McDonald & Burton, 2002). One reason for this could be the growth in foreign exchange activity that leads to less effective levels of central bank intervention. In fact, the current volume of foreign exchange transactions on any single day exceeds the combined values of reserves held at all central banks (Madura, 1995). In this context, work by Madura and Tucker (1991) also showed that the market believed that coordinated central bank intervention would not stabilize foreign exchange markets. Hence, 1993 saw the end of the EMS. Since this time, a new scenario of increasing floating exchange rates has begun.

In this scenario, the main problems that multinational companies have been facing are exchange rate risk, differential inflation rates among their major trading partners, and volatile exchange rates leading to changes in the prices of products (McDonald & Burton, 2002). In this sense, Buckley and Casson (1998) recognised that 'following the breakdown of the Bretton Woods system, exchange rate fluctuations have created a new dimension of financial volatility' where 'every national subsidiary of a MNE experiences a multiplicity of shocks from around the world'.

2.10 Conclusion

A detailed discussion of how the exchange rate risk affects the international operations of companies will be presented in the next chapter. Nevertheless, in order to conclude this chapter, it is important to state that this type of risk is a major concern for countries with less developed financial markets (compared to those in the European Union, the United States, or Japan), and for companies (especially small and medium-sized enterprises) with restricted access to global financial services and/or fewer resources to implement and monitor an active hedging programme.

3

Review of the Literature

3.1 Introduction

This chapter presents an analysis of the literature on the different fields related to this work – first, on the internationalization of companies and, secondly, on the foreign exchange rate risk exposure. Then section 3.4 assesses the different methods to measure the foreign exchange exposure. The chapter also introduces the main argument of this work – that a holistic approach is needed to minimize the effects of the foreign exchange exposure.

3.2 A review of the main conceptual frameworks on the internationalization of companies

Following the introduction presented in the previous chapter explaining the current situation of international trade and foreign investments, it is important to analyse the main theories behind companies' overseas investments. In this context, *The Future of the Multinational Enterprise* (Buckley & Casson, 1976) identified the 'juxtaposition' of two strands of economic theory that take the firm as a main unit of analysis and became the starting point of one of the dominant conceptual frameworks on the multinational enterprise (Dunning, 2003). First, considering the firm as an exchange function, Buckley and Casson's multinational enterprise 'is concerned primarily with why single firms internalise product markets' and by doing so how they benefit from the reduction of transaction costs. Secondly, analysing the company as a value-adding unit, the multinational enterprise's objective 'is to increase value added in the most cost-effective way' by performing tasks that are unique to this firm as 'the market itself cannot undertake the transformation function'. As a result, the combination of these exchange and value-adding functions determine the profitability of the company along with its growth prospects (Dunning, 2003).

In this context, Dunning (2003) said that before the 1950s 'there was little overlap between the two approaches'. It was then, between the 1950s and the 1970s, that 'signs of an implicit incorporation of the market internationalisation approach in the value-added approach' can be found. Dunning also added that foreign direct investment (FDI) theory developed in the late 1960s and 1970s (Caves, 1971, 1974; Hymer, 1960, 1968; McManus, 1972; Vernon, 1966, 1974) had an important influence on Buckley and Casson's work by adding a 'cross-border geographical diversification' to the theory of the firm as the authors were 'seeking to explain the activities of firms outside their national boundaries and financed by FDI'. Finally, Dunning stated that also after the 1950s, studies on multinational enterprise became 'increasingly interdisciplinary' with 'organisational or behavioural theorists making an increasingly important contribution'. This was triggered mainly by the poor view of the traditional profit-maximizing company during the 1960s, and by a realization of the importance of 'the way in which firms were actually organised to perform their value-added activities' (Dunning, 2003). Figure 3.1 shows the theoretical developments upon which Buckley and Casson's framework is based.

At the same time that Buckley and Casson presented their work, Dunning (1977) presented what is known as the OLI paradigm, or the eclectic theory. This theory is, in the words of the author, a second stage of enquiry on international business, trying to offer a 'more integrated approach on the why, where, and how' of internationalization activities. As with the Buckley and Casson model, the OLI theory is also a 'juxtaposition' but, in this case, of three interrelated factors rather than of two strands of economic theory. The three factors are:

> (i) the competitive (or O specific) advantages of existing or potential MNEs (inter alia as identified by the resource-based, evolutionary, and organisational theories of the firm), (ii) the locational (or L specific) advantages of particular countries in offering complementary assets, for these advantages to be exploited or augmented, and

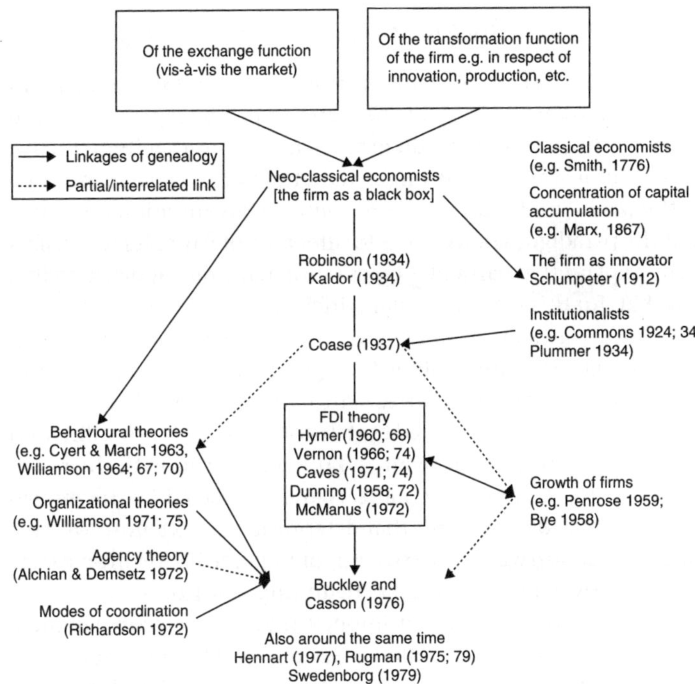

Figure 3.1 Some antecedents of internationalization theory
Source: Dunning (2003).

> (iii) the propensity of the firms possessing the O specific advantages to combine these with those foreign-based assets, by FDI, rather than by (or in addition to) the market mechanism or some kind of non-equity cooperative venture. (Dunning, 2001b)

The years from the late 1980s to the beginning of the twenty-first century saw some new and other complementary explanations to theories of international business activity, in addition to a trend of multidisciplinary research. During this period, three main strands of thinking were recognised (Dunning, 2001b). The first strand argued that companies go abroad or increase their international operations in order to improve their competitive advantages, to create new advantages, and to exploit these advantages (Chen & Chen, 1998; Dunning, 1996; Dunning & Lundan, 1998; Enright, 1998, 2000; Kogut & Zander, 1994; Kuemmerle, 1999; Malmberg et al., 1996; Moon, 1999;

Box 2 Criticism of Dunning's OLI paradigm

Dunning (2001a) has recognised criticisms of the OLI paradigm in four different areas. First, of the claim that the 'explanatory variables identified by the paradigm are so numerous that its predictive value is almost zero', Dunning said that each OLI variable included in the paradigm is based on 'economic or organisational theory', that the paradigm's objective is to offer a set of variables to satisfactorily explain the 'particular types of foreign value-added activity', and that, for this reason, similar criticism could be applied to other 'general theories of FDI and MNE activity'. Secondly, to the suggestion that 'it is misleading to suggest that the triumvirate of variables which make up the eclectic paradigm are independent of one another', Dunning stated that 'it is the successful coordination of the O advantages of foreign and domestic firms with their own L advantages, and how each affects and is affected by the modality of resource deployment, that determines the extent to which a particular country is able to sustain, or upgrade its wealth-creating capacities over a period of time' (Dunning, 2001a).

The third area of criticism implied that 'the eclectic paradigm insufficiently allows for differences in the strategic response of firms to any given configuration of OLI variables' and that 'the paradigm is couched in static (or comparatively static) terms and offers little guidance as to the dynamics of the internationalisation process of firms'. Dunning responded by saying that 'the strategy followed by firms in response to a given OLI configuration in time t_0 is governed by their desire to protect or influence that configuration in t_1'. Finally, Kojima (1982) presented a fourth criticism of the eclectic paradigm by saying that Dunning's approach, 'and that of the internationalisation scholars, is purely a micro-economic phenomenon' (Dunning, 2001a). Dunning found that these arguments fall down as Kojima 'insists upon applying a strictly neoclassical framework of thought to explain a phenomenon that is outside that framework of thought'.

Solvell & Birkinshaw, 2000; Wesson, 1993, 1997). The second thread focused its research on the forms taken by foreign investments, a strand fuelled mainly by the wave of mergers, acquisitions, joint ventures and alliances which have occurred during this period (Casson, 2000; Kogut & Kulatilaka, 1994). The third strand looked at the inclusion of international non-equity cooperative agreements in the field of international economic involvement: (i) to help firms improve their R&D capabilities; (ii) to use resources and skills available in different parts of the world and coordinate with those internally controlled; and (iii) to benefit from taking part in clusters (Doz et al., 1997; Dunning, 1995; Florida, 1995; Storper & Scott, 1995).

3.3 A review of the literature on foreign exchange rate risk exposure

This section, and following sub-sections, present an analysis at the company level of how international firms are affected by the variations in the exchange rate with some references to the specific situation in emerging markets. As suggested in Chapter 1 and, following the findings of Aggarwal and Soenen (1989) in the US, the main argument of this work is that a holistic approach, considering decisions from different areas within the company, is needed to protect the value of investments against the foreign exchange rate risk in emerging markets.

The following review of the literature considers how finance, marketing, operations management, and strategic planning, the functional areas that encompass the holistic approach, are affected by variations in the exchange rate. This analysis is carried out mainly at the company level; however, some references to the industry level are included. This approach can be seen in Figure 3.2.

3.3.1 Finance

Shapiro (2003) defined hedging a particular currency exposure as 'establishing an offsetting currency position so that whatever is lost or gained on the original currency exposure is exactly offset by a corresponding foreign exchange gain or loss on the currency hedge'. In addition, this author stated that 'the most important aspect of foreign exchange risk management is to incorporate currency change expectations into all basic corporate decisions' (Shapiro, 2003). To

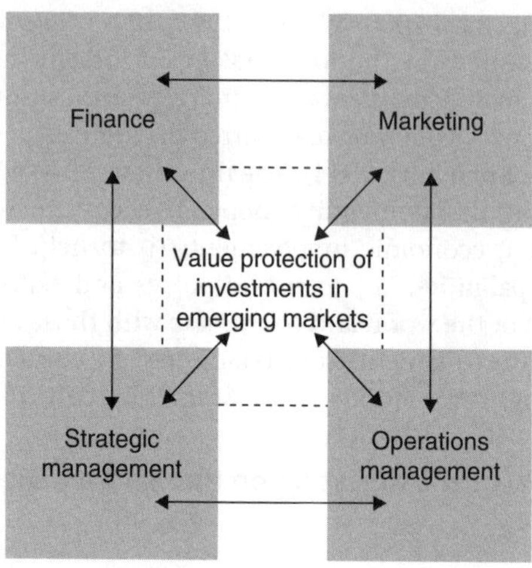

Figure 3.2 A holistic approach

incorporate such risks it is necessary to analyse how foreign exchange variations affect companies. This is presented in Table 3.1, which shows a comparison between the different types of exposure: translation, transaction, and operating exposure. As can be seen, these exposures cannot always be precisely separated but instead overlap to some extent.

Table 3.1 suggests that the most relevant problem is transaction exposure since this has a real and measurable effect on cash flows. For this reason, companies use several instruments to minimize their effects. Examples of these instruments are the Futures Contract, where a company is entitled to receive a specified amount in a specified currency for a stated price on a specified date. This instrument is used mostly for small amounts. A second example is the Forward Hedge, which involves a forward contract that specifies the exchange rate at which currencies will be exchanged. It is common with large amounts. A third example is the hedge in the Money Market, which involves taking a money market position to cover future payables or receivables. A fourth example is the Currency Option Hedge, where a company purchases a currency call/put option that represents the currency and the amount related to payables or receivables (Madura, 1995). These tools are mostly used for short-term hedging.

Table 3.1 A comparison of translation, transaction, and operating exposure

Translation exposure Changes in income statement items and the book value of balance sheet assets and liabilities that are caused by an exchange rate change. The resulting exchange gains and losses are determined by accounting rules and are paper only. The measurement of accounting exposure is retrospective in nature as it is based on activities that occurred in the past. *Impacts: balance sheet assets and liabilities and income statement items that already exist*	**Operating exposure** Changes in the amount of future operating cash flows caused by an exchange rate change. The resulting exchange gains or losses are determined by changes in the firm's future competitive position and are real. The measurement of operating exposure is prospective in nature as it is based on future activities. *Impacts: revenues and costs associated with future sales*
Transaction exposure Changes in the value of outstanding foreign currency-denominated contracts (that is, contracts that give rise to future foreign currency cash flows) that are brought about by a change in the exchange rate. The resulting exchange gains and losses are determined by the nature of the contracts already entered into and are real. The measurement of transaction exposure mixes the retrospective and prospective because it is based upon activities that occurred in the past but will be settled in the future. Contracts already on the balance sheet are part of accounting exposure, whereas contracts not yet on the balance sheet are part of operating exposure. *Impacts: contracts already entered into, but... to be settled at a later date*	
Economic exposure The two cash-flow exposures – operating exposure and transaction exposure – combine to equal a company's economic exposure. In technical terms, economic exposure is the extent to which the value of the firm – as measured by the present value of its expected cash flows – will change when exchange rates change.	

Source: Adapted from Shapiro (2003).

On the other hand, Madura (1995) stated that in order to hedge long-term transaction exposure, firms need to be capable of attempting an accurate estimate of foreign currency payables or receivables that will occur several years hence. In this kind of situation, Long-term Forward Contracts are suitable for firms that have set up fixed-price exporting or importing contracts over a long period. Another technique could be Currency Swap, where two firms arrange a future exchange of, for example, British pounds for US dollars in five years at a negotiated exchange rate. A third example is the strategy of Parallel Loan, where two parties can exchange currencies with a promise to re-exchange these currencies at a specified exchange rate at a future date.

Alternatively, when one or more of these hedge tools are not available to eliminate transaction exposure, firms can consider another method to reduce their exposure (Madura, 1995). For example, leading and lagging, which mean adjustments in the timing of movements of money to reflect expectations about future currency variations. Another option could be a cross-hedge, that is, a forward contract on a currency highly positively correlated to the one needed. A third alternative may be a diversification to currencies that are not highly positively correlated.

Finally, in order to reduce the level of operating exposure, companies could increase/decrease sales in new or existing foreign markets as well as augmenting/diminishing their dependency on foreign suppliers. Furthermore, they can establish or eliminate production facilities in foreign markets, and increase/reduce their level of debt denominated in foreign currencies (Madura, 1995).

Having shown the different options to protect their assets, Doherty and Smith (2001) added that, in general, the companies' aim when managing these exposures should be to avoid reductions in their operating value, that is, 'reductions in the present value of expected operating cash flows'. In this context, Shapiro (2003) also said that a sensible objective for an exchange risk management strategy should be 'to protect the dollar [home currency] earning power of the company as a whole'. To accomplish these objectives, the role of financial management should be to structure the firm's liabilities in such a way that 'the reduction in asset earnings is matched by a corresponding decrease in the cost of servicing these liabilities'. However, 'this approach concentrates exclusively on risk reduction rather than on cost reduction. Where financial market imperfections are significant, a firm might consider exposing itself to more exchange risk in order to lower its expected financing costs' (Shapiro, 2003).

These exposures represent a large challenge for companies operating in an economically integrated world. In order to illustrate some of these challenges, Table 3.2 presents a summary of the economic effects of exchange rate changes on multinational corporations. As can be seen, devaluations and revaluations affect revenues, costs and depreciation in different directions, as well as to different degrees.

3.3.1.1 Economic (or operating) exposure

As presented in Table 3.3, economic exposure can be defined as

> the two cash-flow exposures – operating exposure and transaction exposure – combine to equal a company's economic exposure. In technical terms, economic exposure is the extent to which the value of the firm – as measured by the present value of its expected cash flows – will change when exchange rates change. (Shapiro, 2003)

Other authors do not create an umbrella called economic exposure; they only present transaction exposure on the one hand, and economic (instead of operating) exposure on the other. To illustrate how this exposure affects companies, Table 3.3 describes a pattern of economic exposure.

Economic exposure 'typically has a longer-term time dimension as well as it encompasses the competitive and indirect effects of exchange rate risk' (Martin & Mauer, 2003). The origins of the economic exposure are the changes in the sales prices, sales volumes, and the cost of inputs of the firm and its competitors as the result of exchange rate changes. Since these effects are often indirect, and longer-term in nature, it is unclear if financial hedging is effective (Chow et al., 1997a, 1997b; Pringle, 1991; Pringle & Connolly, 1993). Economic exposure also depends upon the marketing and operations strategies, along with the company's suppliers and potential competitors, in addition to the corporate-level finance unit; therefore, it is complex to assess. Furthermore, Martin and Mauer (2003) added that economic exposure can even affect domestic firms

Table 3.2 Characteristic economic effects of exchange rate changes on multinational corporations

Cashflow categories	Relevant economic factors	Devaluation impact	Revaluation impact
Revenue		Parent-currency revenue impact	Parent-currency revenue impact
Export Sales	Price-sensitive demand	Increase (++)	Decrease (−−)
	Price-insensitive demand	Slight increase (+)	Slight decrease (−)
Local Sales	Weak prior import competition	Sharp decline (−−)	Increase (++)
	Strong prior import competition	Decrease (−) (less than devaluation %)	Slight increase (+)
Costs		Parent-currency cost impact	Parent-currency cost impact
Domestic inputs	Low import content	Decrease (−−)	Increase (++)
	High import content/inputs used in export or import-competing sectors	Slight decrease (−)	Slight increase (+)
Imported inputs	Small local market	Remain the same (0)	Remain the same (0)
	Large local market	Slight decrease (−)	Slight increase (+)
Depreciation		Cashflow impact	Cashflow impact
Fixed assets	No asset valuation adjustment	Decrease by devaluation % (−−)	Increase by revaluation % (++)
	Asset valuation adjustment	Decrease (−)	Increase (+)

Note: To interpret the above table, and taking the impact of a devaluation on local demand as an example, it is assumed that if import competition is weak, local prices will climb slightly, if at all; in such a case, there would be a sharp contraction in parent-company revenue. If imports generate strong competition, local-currency prices are expected to increase, although not to the full extent of the devaluation; in this instance, only a moderate decline in parent-company revenue would be registered.
Source: Shapiro (1977).

(see also Hodder, 1982; Marston, 2001; Pringle, 1995; Shapiro, 1975; von Ungerm-Sternberg & von Weizssacker, 1990).

Some studies stated that geographically-positioned production facilities, sales revenues, suppliers, and funding, could be effective in

Table 3.3 The time pattern of economic exposure

Non-contractual	Quasi-contractual	Contractual	
Investment in new product development, distribution facilities, brand name, marketing, foreign production capacity, foreign supplier relationships	Quote foreign currency price, receive a foreign currency price	Ship product/bill customers in foreign currency, receive bill for supplies in foreign currency	Collect foreign currency receivables, pay foreign currency liabilities

Source: Shapiro (2003).

reducing economic exposure (Bodnar et al., 1998; Chow et al., 1997a, 1997b; George & Schroth, 1991; Jacque, 1981; Jorion, 1990; Lessard & Lightstone, 1986; Martin et al., 1999; Martin & Mauer, 2003; Pantzalis et al., 2001; Pringle, 1995). Norton and Malindretos (1991) concurred, suggesting that economic exposure requires: (i) diversification of production, raw material sources, and operations; and (ii) diversification of financing sources. However, relocating operations to form such hedges can be expensive and difficult to reverse (Chow et al., 1997a; Hodder, 1982; Martin & Mauer, 2003; Pringle & Connolly, 1993). In other words, the costs of geographically diversified production, along with its perceived net benefits, are sometimes not enough to offset the economic exposure. Nevertheless, the CFOs could choose to diversify financing sources since this is relatively cheap compared with diversifying operations.

Another problem when hedging economic exposure is the need for coordination among the functional areas of the company. For example, the complexity of the information required to assess economic exposure may involve different areas. In addition, its long-term nature makes it difficult to identify and measure economic exposure; then 'it is possible that the perceived costs of hedging outweigh the perceived benefits or that the exposure is not recognized, and the economic exposure remains unhedged' (Martin & Mauer, 2003).

3.3.2 Marketing

The price of products sold in emerging markets should consider the risks associated with the investments in these regions. This means that the final price should take into account both the country risk and also the business risk. Country risk comprises factors such as macroeconomic volatility, the potential for regulatory or political change, and poorly-defined property rights and enforcement mechanisms. Similarly, the business risk is attributable to microeconomic factors such as rapid entry and exit rates, changing consumer preferences, industrial structural change, and the possibility of regulatory change (Kennedy, 2002). As these risk premiums should be included in the cost of capital used to discount (future) cash flows, the final price of products should be set at a level that overcomes a cost of capital[1] that is likely to be higher in emerging markets than in developed countries. As a consequence, it is probable that the price of products was higher in riskier markets and, for this reason, a special price strategy for these markets should be considered.

In this sense, McDonald and Burton (2002) added that pricing in international markets is one of the most important strategic decisions for firms. The price strategy has a direct effect on demand as well as on revenues; hence, it is a key determinant in the success of an international venture. They presented three factors that can affect prices. The first factor with great influence in pricing decisions in an international setting is government regulations – that is, minimum and maximum prices. The second factor is that consumer tastes and demands vary widely in different countries, giving companies the opportunity to charge different prices for the same product. They recognised that an experienced marketing team can handle these two concerns successfully. The third factor is currency fluctuation; this relies mostly on the accurate forecasting variations in the value of currencies and other complex techniques which, by its own nature, is not as easily handled by the marketing team.

In this context, Rugman and Hodgetts (2003) defined exchange risk in pricing as 'the probability that a company will be unable to adjust prices and costs to offset changes in the exchange rate'. Within this definition, it would thus be of interest to learn what would happen, for example, if a company with production facilities overseas were not capable of imposing a new (relatively) higher price that is a consequence of variations in the value of currencies; in other words, if a company cannot alter its costs to compensate for the changes in the exchange rate. Shapiro (2003) expressed this concern with the following questions: 'can the firm maintain its dollar [home currency] margins both at home and abroad?, can the company maintain its dollar [home currency] price on domestic sales in the face of lower-priced foreign imports?, and, in the case of foreign sales, can the firm raise its foreign currency selling price sufficiently to preserve its dollar [home currency] profit margin?'

Prahalad and Lieberthal (2003) introduced another pressure in this direction. They suggested rethinking the price/performance equation as 'consumers in big emerging markets are getting a fast education in global standards but they often are unwilling to pay global prices'. Therefore, price becomes a key marketing issue in emerging markets as the result of its potential effect on consumer demand (Rugman & Hodgetts, 2003) and, as a consequence, on revenues.

In general, two strategies have been used to deal with these price issues. On the one hand, for business-to-business (B2B) relations, Narayandas, Quelch and Swartz (2000) showed that some companies have pressured their suppliers to accept global-pricing contracts. These contracts imply that suppliers of components used in the companies' products charge the same for parts from one region as they do for parts from another, generally using the same currency. On the other hand, in retail marketing, Lowengart and Mizrahi (2000) found that the use of an international reference price has proved to be useful during long periods of currency instability. These authors mentioned the example of Israel between 1981 and 1985, when retailers indicated prices in terms of US dollars because the Israeli Shekel was not considered to be a reliable currency. Nevertheless, these two strategies put the exchange rate risk only on one side of the business relation (buyer or supplier, depending upon the slope of the demand and supply curves); in other words, the most powerful part sets the conditions. Consequently, these price policies are not a long-term solution.

The analysis in the marketing field needs to be complemented with the other two Ps: promotion and product. On the one hand, Madura (1995) said that it is difficult to find a unique and standardized hedge to protect money that is already invested in promotion because this depends mainly upon the accounting procedures that companies use when consolidating financial statement data – especially when these procedures are linked to government regulations. In other words, this is a translation exposure and the resulting gains or losses are determined by accounting rules and are paper only. However, it is difficult to imagine managers keen to show 'paper losses', especially if they mean lower book values for their companies.

On the product side, the exchange rate can affect companies in at least two ways. The first way is in the payment of royalties/licences to a third company (which could also be a parent company) that owns the rights to exploit a product. This contractual economic (transaction) exposure can be hedged using the tools described in the previous section. However, as shown before, this protection is insufficient when a company cannot estimate its payables accurately – a typical situation when talking about sales that will occur several years hence.

The second way in which exchange rates can affect companies operating in emerging markets is through the development of new products. Work by Madura (1995) presented some strategies to protect this non-contractual economic exposure – for example, decreasing sales in foreign markets or eliminating production facilities abroad. Nevertheless, these options are not always possible, especially when a company has established a wholly-owned subsidiary abroad. On the contrary, in this case the company should be trying to develop new products to better serve the local market and, consequently, to increase its market share. This latter option was mentioned by Quelch (2003), who showed that many companies in emerging markets have started to include the opinions of local business partners in their decisions about the adaptation of product attributes to local tastes. At the same time, Quelch continued, companies have changed their structures to allow local managers to have more authority over product development and marketing. These findings seems to be in line with the concept of 'being local' and also with Prahalad and Lieberthal's (2003) proposition of serving emerging markets with local developments. In this sense, these authors suggested that 'some redesign is often necessary to reflect differences in use and distribution, even when customers in emerging markets appear to want the same products sold elsewhere'. For example, they mentioned the case of Fiat, which 'designed a new model called the Palio specifically for Brazilians, and the company is now poised to transfer that success from Brazil to India'. These movements, from globally standardized to locally adapted/developed products, contrast with the classic view of global markets presented by Levitt (1983). In fact, Quelch, Prahalad, and Lieberthal presented evidence that global-brand owners are buying local brands (along with local products) in emerging markets.

3.3.3 Operations management

One report from UNCTAD (2002) stated that international production is expected to continue growing as transnational corporations expand their role in the increasingly globalized world economy. This expansion is affecting different effects upon the industries and countries affected. In this sense, the report mentioned three main forces that lead this process. First, policy liberalization opened national markets to be recipients of FDI flows. Secondly, rapid technological changes made it economical to integrate distant operations and move products across markets in the search for efficiency. Thirdly, increasing competition induced companies to search for new ways to increase their efficiency (UNCTAD, 2002). Furthermore, UNCTAD mentioned a number of studies also indicating that companies will continue their international expansion. 'More specifically, they [the studies] suggest that the most preferred destinations will include large developed-country markets, as well as a number of key destinations in developing countries (especially China, Brazil, Mexico, and South Africa).' These research works, along with the increasing development of local products presented above, imply that facilities located overseas are likely to continue growing.

In this context, it is important to highlight that multinational production planning is complex, usually takes place over several years, and involves significant capital expenditures. One of the problems with planning is that, once put in place, errors in implementing or changing facilities can be costly (Breitman & Lucas, 1987). For these reasons, most multinational companies have dedicated planning departments that are continually evaluating several alternatives as well as different regulatory regimes to determine the most appropriate location to install a production facility. In this sense, companies should look for benefits from operating across different regulatory systems (Ietto-Gillies, 2000). For example, companies can be benefited when their activities allow them to invoice their internal transfers in such a way as to minimize their worldwide taxation liabilities. Another source of benefits in a multi-regime environment for companies could be a fragmented labour force as, in the short-to-medium term, this may result in lower labour costs at the level of the firm as a whole (Ietto-Gillies, 2000). A third example could be a risk minimization strategy – that is, a reduction in the risk of disruption to production as a consequence of multinational spread production and labour fragmentation. Within this last case, Ietto-Gillies (2000) suggested that 'operating in many countries may also diminish the risk (or increase the opportunities) linked to possible changes in currencies'. In this context, for instance, many Japanese electronics firms transferred some of their manufacturing capacity to other locations overseas before 1995 (when dealing with a strong Yen) which helped Japanese manufacturers diversify exchange risks (Financial Times, 1996).

Huchzermeier and Cohen (1996) said that this risk minimization strategy is achieved mainly through supply flexibility, which is included in the design of products; as well as operational flexibility, which is embedded in the design of the supply chain network. Furthermore, Cohen and Lee (1989) added that the degree of this operational flexibility will determine a company's manufacturing competitiveness as it allows a multinational company to exploit comparative costs differentials on a global scale. Following these principles, for example, in 2000, Volkswagen introduced a modular manufacturing system after having identified 11 modules in the design of its products which could be shared among different platforms (Kubes & Rädler, 2003).

Huchzermeier (1993) proposed the use of this operational flexibility as a hedge tool against the MNC's exchange risk exposure. This approach is called operational hedging. The rationale behind it is that the MNC can maximize 'its expected, discounted, global, after-tax value through the exercise of supply chain network options and/or through exploitation of operational flexibility contingent on exchange rate realizations' (Huchzermeier & Cohen, 1996). However, on the downside, 'the costs of operational hedging are determined by the switching costs and fixed operating costs of maintaining (excess) capacity' (Huchzermeier & Cohen, 1996). In order to assess its efficiency, Huchzermeier and Cohen presented a model to value operational hedging showing that this strategy could be potentially beneficial in increasing the firm's value; however, its empirical relevance to MNCs with a network of manufacturing operations in emerging markets is still the subject of further research.

On the other hand, a study by Baron (1976) showed that, in general, exports tended to be invoiced in the currency of the importing – rather than the producing – country. This finding is in line with global pricing presented in section 3.3.2. Therefore, the importer transferred all the risk of a price change as the result of movements in the exchange rate to the producer. In other words, the buyer defined competition for suppliers. Consequently, the manner in which price changes are dealt with resulted in continuous confrontations and negotiations. Such practices can be wasteful in the long term, as they could lead to poor supply and, consequently, higher costs (Lamming, 1993).

In an attempt to avoid these problems, Lamming (1993) presented Lean Supply, the fifth phase of a 'five-phase model of customer–supplier relations'. Specifically, the author proposed a strategic model for assembler–supplier relationships in the automotive industry. In dealing with price changes, this model introduced the need to exchange information between buyer and supplier in order to obtain a higher degree of cooperation combined with transparency in costing. Then, in Lean Supply, the process of achieving a new price of equilibrium 'is incorporated and blended with the need for mutual benefit. Thus, as material supply or economic forces cost increases on the supplier, it is the joint responsibility of the partners to find ways to counteract the problem' – for example, reducing the use of the material that increased the price, or reducing another cost to compensate.

The Lean Supply Model's answer to the exchange rate risk can be found in the management of capacity section. This section stated that the travel time between supplier and customer is the critical factor in providing Just-in-Time delivery and synchronized manufacture (Lamming, 1993). In fact, Lamming recognized that international borders present a particular challenge with regard to this issue. The VW plant in Rosende, Brazil, seemed to have followed Lean Supply as it was set up along with seven leading suppliers (Kubes & Rädler, 2003). Another example could be General Motors' Gravatai plant, also in Brazil, where the company had gone 'a step further by designing the plant and the car it produces in conjunction with seventeen suppliers' (Burt, 2001). As a consequence of this joint venture, suppliers relate their own business to the sales market of their customer (Lamming, 1993), i.e. they share destinies. Then, what would happen if exchange rate movements affect the final product's market? This is not a strange question as, for instance, GM stated that the car produced at Gravatai 'is suited to Brazil and neighbouring Mercosur countries' (Burt, 2001). Therefore, changes in the currency value in Brazil, Argentina, Uruguay, or Paraguay and additionally in Chile and Bolivia could not only affect GM's cash flow, but also expose the 17 main suppliers to transaction, economic and translation risk. For the reasons mentioned above, it is not clear how Lean Supply proposes to deal with a floating exchange rate environment and its associated variations in the value of currencies.

3.3.4 Strategic planning

Hedging and strategic planning are present in both the planning stage and also the day-to-day management of an international company. In this sense, Kennedy (1984) suggested that multinational companies should focus upon two issues: (i) assessing the foreign exchange risk inherent in overseas investments versus the expected returns; and (ii) linking the strategic planning of parent companies to that of their foreign affiliate. Lees and Mauer (2002) presented this situation from a different perspective; they said that 'managing economic exposures also typically requires cross-functional coordination within the MNC, which is frequently difficult to achieve given the different professional orientations of such disparate groups as the treasury department, marketing, and production management within the MNC'.

In terms of strategic decisions, Miller and Reuer (1998) found that 'foreign market participation through direct investment reduces firms' exposures to exchange rate movements'. Furthermore, Porter (1990) said that firms engaging in differentiation strategies have more sustainable competitive advantages than cost leaders under conditions of currency volatility. Product differentiation created by investments in 'higher order' advantages (for example, proprietary technology, unique product characteristics, or brand reputation) strengthens the firm's capability to pass through to customers the changes in costs due to currency movements. Passing on cost increases to customers is not feasible using a cost leadership strategy in the presence of competing firms with lower costs sourcing opportunities. In line with Porter's opinion, Sundaram and Mishra (1991) and Sundaram and Black (1992) proposed that a firm's ability to pass through currency rate fluctuations to customers depends on the price elasticity of customer demand, which, in turn, depends on the degree of product differentiation.

Nevertheless, Kennedy (1984) stated that 'foreign exchange rate always has some impact on multinational companies' financial statements', regardless of the companies' ability to 'circumvent the imperfections in the international markets by gaining control over foreign production or marketing'. For example, Lees and Mauer (2002) stated that 'exposure can be reduced by geographically positioning production, sales, sourcing, and financing operations; however, relocating operations solely to hedge exchange rate exposure can be expensive'. In other words, the ability to operate internationally does not ensure that companies can compete and become profitable in the global marketplace.

At the industry level, Miller and Reuer (1998) hypothesized that MNCs should study the industry in which they are competing in order to assess their exposure. This is mainly because 'firm's exposures are also contingent on the strategies of competing firms' as companies with sales only in their national markets could also suffer from economic exposure. This exposure can come from imported parts or final products competing in the same market. In addition, multinational companies could cross-subsidize markets by exploiting the shifts in the exchange rate affecting, as a result, the domestic firm's competitive position. In other words, companies should 'consider not only the extent to which the firm sells its products in international markets, but also the extent to which intercountry rivalry affects the industry'. In a very specific situation – US manufacturing firms using the US dollar and the currencies of their main trading partner – they did not find evidence that intercountry rivalry at the industry level increases firms' economic exposure. However, it could be worth studying their hypothesis in a broader context – for example, European or Japanese companies using many different currencies.

Hakkarainen et al. (1998) found that 'most empirical studies about foreign exchange exposure management practices concentrate on the behaviour of multinational corporations that are located in the United States of America and in the United Kingdom. Studies about practices of firms located in smaller open economies are rather limited' (but see Batten et al., 1993; Oxelheim, 1984). As a result, Hakkarainen et al. supported the need to study Finnish industrial firms as:

> (i) their exposure management practices can be considered to be at a comparatively early stage of financial development since Finnish firms have not traditionally been influenced in international financial markets, and (ii) it is possible that Finnish managers' attitudes to risk and their foreign exchange hedging

strategies may have been influenced by recent upheavals and transformation in the Finnish financial markets.

These two considerations can also be applied to other European countries and their companies; for example, to the internationalization processes of Spanish or Portuguese companies, as well as to French or Italian utility companies previously owned by the state. Their conclusions showed that

> the length of time since the firm developed a formal corporate hedging policy is associated with the degree to which exposures are hedged. Most firms (56% of their study) which developed a formal foreign exchange policy within the last two to five years hedge both transaction and translation exposures to a great extent. Firms which developed a foreign exchange policy within the last two years tend to hedge translation exposure fully, and monitor rather than hedge economic exposure.

3.4 Main approaches to assessing the impact of variations in the exchange rate

Section 3.3 reviewed the effects of variations in the exchange rate on four areas of management. This section attempts to show how these effects can be assessed and measured.

Many empirical studies focusing on the exchange rate exposure of companies use variations of what is known as the market-based model, which analyses the effects of variations in the exchange rate on stock returns (Allayannis et al., 2001; Bartov & Bodnar, 1994; Choi & Prasad, 1995; Faff & Marshall, 2005; Fornes & Cardoza, 2009; He & Ng, 1998; Jorion, 1990; Martin et al., 1999). The election of this model is based upon the possibility of assessing the overall impact of changes in the currency price on the value of the firm, its flexibility, and its forward-looking nature. However, this model has some limitations when estimating and managing exchange rate exposure. First, 'by using the capital market to assess exposure, there is heavy reliance upon the market to accurately use available information' (Martin & Mauer, 2003). For example, Bartov and Bodnar (1994) said that investors might not use all of the available information to evaluate the impact of exchange rate changes on firm value. In addition,

Chow, Lee, and Solt (1997b) stated that investors are unable to assess the impact on firm value from current exchange rate changes because they found a greater frequency of significant exposure using long-horizon returns. Furthermore, both Marshall and Weetman (2002) and Roulstone (1999) argued that inadequate financial statement disclosures on the extent of exposure contribute to the impedance of the capital market in its efforts to assess exposure. Secondly, the market-based model 'does not provide a sense of the time profile of exchange rate effects. Whether such effects impact company operations in the short term or in a longer-term time frame is a major issue for many analysts, investors, and managers' (Martin & Mauer, 2003).

In comparison, other studies use what is called the cash-flow-based approach where the main focus is the sensitivity of the company's cash flow to variations in the exchange rate (Fornes & Cardoza, 2005; Ho Park et al., 2006). The main benefits of this approach are: (i) it does not rely on the assumption that the market can accurately measure the impact of variations in the value of the currency on cash flows; in fact, with this approach it could be possible to identify patterns of cash flows' reactions to such variations; (ii) the market participants do not need to know and use all the available information on how a company could be affected by movements in the exchange rate; (iii) this method allows corporate financial managers, investors, analysts, etc. to understand the nature of the exposure by separating the short-term and long-term effects of exchange rate risk; this is important as different causes need different hedging strategies; and (iv) companies are concerned about the stability of their cash flow and how it could be affected by variations in the exchange rate mainly by its implications for credit ratings.

The main weakness of these models is that they only measure net impacts, i.e. the remaining exposure after the company's hedging activities.

> As a result, it is difficult to empirically detect exchange rate exposure using either approach. In other words, sensitivity of stock returns or cash flows to exchange rate risk may not be significant for firms that have ex ante exposures but that are proficiently managing these exposures. (Martin & Mauer, 2003)

For this reason, this work also proposes the study of the exposure to exchange rate through an analysis of the decisions taken (in previous periods) by companies to hedge their assets. In addition, to assess the effectiveness of these decisions, it would be necessary to study the relation between the decisions and the impact of the variations in the exchange rate on cash flows or stock returns.

3.4.1 Other alternatives for measuring economic exposure and hedging

Kennedy (1984) proposed the analysis of what he called the financial and the natural exposures. The 'financial exposure is a measure of the extent to which a company has chosen to protect itself from what happens overseas'. The 'natural exposure is a measure of the extent to which companies leave themselves vulnerable to economic conditions overseas by doing business in foreign currency'. Then, the companies' exposure can be determined 'by deducting financial exposure (the dollars [home currency] the MNC preserves through hedges) from natural exposure (the dollars [home currency] the corporation gains or loses through operating policies and if foreign currency devaluation does not equal inflation)'.

Miller and Reuer (1998) stated that 'the relation of export sales intensity to economic exposure considers not only the value of receivables, but also the effect of foreign exchange rate movements on future sales' and that this 'export intensity would ideally be measured as net export intensity (i.e. exports less imports divided by total sales)'.

Shapiro and Rutenberg (1974) presented another point of view. They suggested that before making a decision about when to hedge and, therefore, measuring their exposure, companies need to identify what they call the most suitable subsidiaries. This suitability depends upon: (i) 'the national tax treatment of foreign exchange losses and hedging costs and gains; for example, can the gains be categorized as capital gains and what is their tax rate?'; (ii) 'the individual tax status of the national subsidiary in that year (with the possibility of losses carried forward and back)'; and (iii) 'how the government of the headquarters nation will tax this gain or loss abroad'. They supported this suggestion by saying that 'only after-tax costs are relevant to a hedging decision'.

Hagelin and Pramborg (2004) found a 'relationship between firm size and foreign exchange exposure, namely that the smaller the firm, the larger the exposure in absolute terms'. They explain this finding by saying that it could reflect previous evidence found between the size of the firm and the use of financial hedging (Bodnar et al., 1998). They also stated that large companies are likely to be operating in different countries and, as a consequence, using many different currencies; this multinational operation could be used as an operational hedge in comparison with smaller firms that are likely to be exporters or importers with fewer opportunities to apply operational hedgings.

Finally, Miller and Reuer (1998) found that previous research in finance focused on industries or portfolios of firms from various industries (Amihud, 1994; Bodnar & Gentry, 1993; Donnelly & Sheehy, 1996). They said that

> a potential shortcoming of studies examining the economic exposure of industries or multi-industry portfolios is that such aggregations of firms may mask differences in firm-specific strategies affecting foreign exchange exposures...The implicit assumption in models aggregating firms at the industry level is that no heterogeneity exists within industries. However, intra-industry heterogeneity is a fundamental premise of strategy research.

These measurements, as shown above, have been applied to several research works. Their use depends mainly upon the focus of the enquiry; in addition, they have presented alternative options to the more widely used methodologies presented in section 3.4. For example, aggregate studies, such as those carried out at the industry level in the 1990s, could be effective in measuring the economic exposure of a group of companies with highly-related value chains, like those companies belonging to a cluster. Therefore, future studies of economic exposure may benefit through the inclusion of any of these methodologies as a complement of the market-based and cash flow-based models.

3.5 Variations in the exchange rate and their effect on the functional areas: a summary

The review of the literature presented above (sections 3.3 and 3.4) showed the areas where variations in the exchange rate can affect companies. A summary of this review can be found in Table 3.4.

Table 3.4 A summary of what is presented by the literature

Finance		
Variations in the exchange rate generate translation, operating, and economic exposures.		(Shapiro, 2003)
Financial instruments are useful mainly for hedging short term.		(Madura, 1995)
Long-term hedging could be done if it is possible to accurately estimate future cash flows.		(Madura, 1995)
Objectives of the financial area the regarding hedging.	Protect home currency earning power of company as a whole.	(Shapiro, 2003)
	Avoid reductions in the present value of expected operating cash flows.	(Doherty & Smith, 2001)
Economic exposure	Has a long-term dimension and the effectiveness of financial hedging against this exposure is unclear.	(Chow et al., 1997a, 1997b; Pringle, 1991; Pringle & Connolly, 1993)
	Includes competitive and indirect effects, and needs coordination among different areas in the company.	(Martin & Mauer, 2003)
	Can affect domestic firms too.	(Martin & Mauer, 2003), (Hodder, 1982; Marston, 2001; Pringle, 1995; Shapiro, 1975; von Ungerm-Sternberg & von Weizssacker, 1990)
	Geographically-positioned production facilities, sales revenues, supplies, and financing operations can be effective for reducing economic exposure.	(Bodnar et al., 1998; Chow et al., 1997a, 1997b; George & Schroth, 1991; Jacque, 1981; Jorion, 1990; Lessard & Lightstone, 1986; Martin et al., 1999; Pantzalis et al., 2001; Pringle, 1995)
	Relocation to hedge operations can be expensive and difficult to reverse.	(Chow et al., 1997a; Hodder, 1982; Pringle & Connolly, 1993)

Marketing		
Price of products sold in emerging markets should consider the risks associated with the investments in these regions.		(Kennedy, 2002)
Price strategy is a key determinant in the success of an international venture. Three factors affect prices.	Government regulations	(McDonald & Burton, 2002)
	Consumer tastes and demands	
	Currency fluctuations.	
Exchange rate risk in pricing.	'The probability that a company will be unable to adjust prices and costs to offset changes in the exchange rate'.	(Rugman & Hodgetts, 2003)
Strategies commonly used to deal with exchange rate changes. These strategies put the exchange rate risk only on one side of the business relation.	Global-pricing contracts.	(Narayandas et al., 2000)
	Use of international reference price.	(Lowengart & Mizrahi, 2000)
Investments in promotion are a translation exposure and depend on accounting procedures.		(Madura, 1995)
Increasing investments in product development in/for emerging markets are likely to increase the need to find a hedging strategy.		(Quelch, 2003)
Operations management		
International production is expected to continue growing.		(UNCTAD, 2002)
Multinational production looks for benefits from operating in different regulatory systems in three different areas.	Invoice internal transfers to minimize worldwide taxation liabilities.	(Ietto-Gillies, 2000)
	Fragmented labour force.	
	Risk minimization strategy (mainly risk of disruption to production).	

(Continued)

Table 3.4 (Continued)

Operational hedging: operational flexibility and supply flexibility as a hedge tool.		(Cohen & Lee, 1989; Huchzermeier, 1993; Huchzermeier & Cohen, 1996; Kubes & Rädler, 2003)
Invoicing exports in the importer's currency.	The importer transferred all the risk to the producer.	(Baron, 1976)
	Could be wasteful, and lead to poor supply and higher costs.	(Lamming, 1993)
Lean Supply	Strategic model for assembler–supplier relationships.	(Lamming, 1993)
	Price of equilibrium incorporated and blended with the need for mutual benefit.	
	International borders present a challenge for this model.	
	Suppliers and assemblers share destinies.	
	Questions over the effects of exchange rate movements on this integrated chain	
Strategic planning		
Multinational companies should assess the risk of their investments overseas and link the strategic planning of the parent and the subsidiaries.		(Kennedy, 1984)
Cross-functional coordination within the company is needed: treasury, marketing, and production.		(Lees & Mauer, 2002)
Foreign direct investment reduces the firm's exposure to exchange rate movements.		(Miller & Reuer, 1998)
A strategy of differentiation strengthens the firm's capability to pass through to customers the changes in costs due to currency movements.		(Porter, 1990)
The company's ability to pass through currency rate fluctuations depends on the price elasticity.		(Sundaram & Black, 1992; Sundaram & Mishra, 1991)

Analysis at the industry level may mask differences in firms' strategies to deal with foreign exchange exposure.	(Miller & Reuer, 1998)
Companies should study the industry in which they are competing in order policy to assess their exposure.	(Miller & Reuer, 1998)
'The length of time since the firm developed a formal corporate hedging is associated with the degree to which exposures are hedged'	(Hakkarainen et al., 1998)
Main approaches to assessing the impact of variations in the exchange rate	
Market-based model	(Allayannis et al., 2001; Bartov & Bodnar, 1994; Choi & Prasad, 1995; Faff & Marshall, 2005; He & Ng, 1998; Jorion, 1990; Martin et al., 1999)
Cashflow-based model	(Fornes & Cardoza, 2006; Ho Park et al., 2006)
Other alternatives for measuring economic exposure	
Financial exposure – natural exposure = company's exposure.	(Kennedy, 1984)
'Time series data as the coefficient computed by regressing shareholder returns on the percentage change in a foreign exchange rate.'	(Miller & Reuer, 1998)
Find the most suitable subsidiary: national tax treatment regarding foreign exchange losses and gains, the tax status of the subsidiary, and how the parent company will tax this gain/loss abroad. 'Only after-tax costs are relevant to a hedging decision.'	(Shapiro & Rutenberg, 1974)
'The smaller the firm, the larger the exposure in absolute terms.'	(Hagelin & Pramborg, 2004)
'Foreign exchange rate always has some impact on companies' financial statements.'	(Kennedy, 1984)

3.6 Conclusion

This chapter reviewed the literature on the fields related to this study. The first part discussed the literature that deals with the internationalization of companies, and the second half analysed the literature on foreign exchange exposure from four different perspectives: finance, marketing, operations management, and strategic planning. Different methods to assess this exposure were also presented. This chapter also introduced the main proposal of this work, that a holistic approach is needed to deal with foreign exchange exposure. The next chapter will present the main conceptual framework of this work.

4
Conceptual Framework and Objectives

4.1 Introduction

The conceptual framework used in this book has been constructed by merging two main streams – the findings from previous works on foreign exchange exposure and on the operations of MNEs in international contexts – as they analyse the same problem of the impacts of the variations in the exchange rate on companies but from different perspectives. The first one, the finance perspective, considers the relationship between these variations and the firms' cash flow. The second one looks at the same relationship from the perspective of operations management, and marketing, and strategic planning. The resulting framework offers a more comprehensive picture of the firms' international activities and how they are affected by movements in the value of currencies. Figure 4.1 shows these two main streams that together create the main conceptual framework. It also shows the context in which this work has being carried out: the emerging markets (whose characteristics were described in sections 2.6 and 2.8) and the increasing economic integration (analysed in sections 2.3 and 2.5).

4.1.1 The finance perspective

The main finance perspective was described in section 3.3.1. Nevertheless, the increasing importance of emerging markets as recipients of foreign direct investments from developed countries calls for specific studies on foreign exchange exposure. This is mainly because it is usually claimed that these markets present a different environment than that of developed economies; therefore, companies' strategies

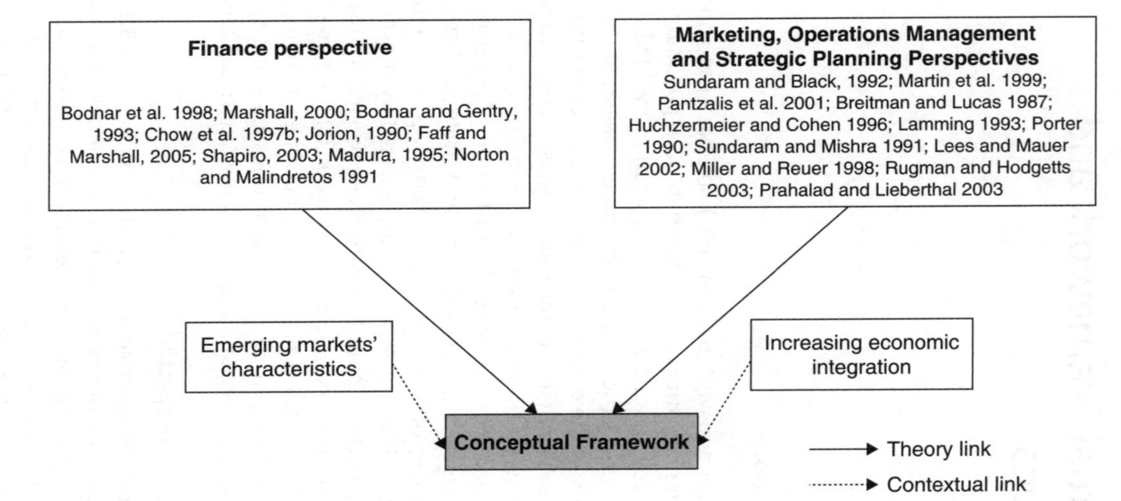

Figure 4.1 Origins and context of the conceptual framework

to deal with this risk may be different. On the other hand, foreign exchange exposure is one of the many risks faced by multinational enterprises and has become an important area of research as well as a source of concern for companies.

The main question has been – and still is – the relation between the unexpected variations in the exchange rate and the changes – lagged or contemporaneous – in the value of firms. This relation has been widely studied in US companies where the results have shown weak evidence (see, for example, Bodnar & Gentry, 1993; Chow et al., 1997a; Dominguez & Tesar, 2001; Jorion, 1990), suggesting an apparent inconsistency among the evidence, the predictions, and the hedging instruments. Other works which have attempted to explain this contradiction have studied this relationship from different perspectives; for example, Choi and Kim (2003), De Jong et al. (2002), Doukas et al. (2001), and Nguyen and Faff (2003) studied companies in other developed countries, Shin and Soenen (1999) used refined measures of FX, Martin et al. (1999) and Pantzalis et al. (2001) tried to assess the operational hedge's effect on the value of firms, Bodnar et al. (1998) and Marshall (2000) analysed the use of hedging instruments in the protection of firms' value, and Faff and Marshall (2005) looked for the determinants of foreign exchange rate exposure of multinational corporations. However, there are only a small number of studies that make specific references to emerging markets.

4.1.2 Marketing, operations management, and strategic planning perspective

This perspective collects the conclusions from previous works (Breitman & Lucas, 1987; Huchzermeier & Cohen, 1996; Lamming, 1993; Lees & Mauer, 2002; Martin et al., 1999; Miller & Reuer, 1998; Pantzalis et al., 2001; Porter, 1990; Prahalad & Lieberthal, 2003; Rugman & Hodgetts, 2003; Sundaram & Mishra, 1991) and are summarized in the work by Sundaram and Black (1992).

Sundaram and Black (1992) recognised that a basic characteristic of the environmental context that multinational enterprises face is the manifestations of 'the relative authority of the sovereign state over exchange rates, politics, culture, regulations, and languages'. From these manifestations, they derived 'two specific attributes of the environment' that are unique for multinational enterprises: (i) 'multiple

Box 3 Sundaram and Black's framework: a summary

Multiple sources of external authority (MA) refers to the multinational company's exposure to the sovereignty of different states and their 'authority to influence events within its legal territory' and their 'choice of being relatively immune to outside influences'. In other words, multinational companies are exposed to 'multiple (and often conflicting) sources of external authority'. In this context, the distinctive characteristic of the environment where multinational companies operate 'arises at the intersection of differences in country environments' where 'in the absence of commonly applicable and enforceable institutional mechanisms, all conflicts arising from cross-border transactions at this intersection of differences in sources of external authority create both opportunities and risks'. 'These risks arise not only because of differences between country environments but also because there is no authoritative superstructure to mediate any conflicts that might arise at the intersection of these differences.'

Multiple denominations of value (MV) refers to the fact that 'the firm's cash flows are denominated in different exchange rates' where the main concerns are 'breakdowns in purchasing power parity'. In this sense, the authors recognised that the problem of MV is economic exposure (a concept explained in Table 3.1 above). As in MA, 'economic exposure (or MV) has been a source of both great risks and opportunities' for companies 'since the advent of the floating exchange rate regime'. 'The crucial issue arising from MV is how the firm's cash flows and asset values are affected by unanticipated shifts in real exchange rates of the home country currency against host or competitor country currencies.'

sources of external authority, and (ii) multiple denominations of value'.

The intention of Sundaram and Black's work was to explore the organizational implications and the two environmental variables, MA and MV, in the context of modes of entry, configuration of activities, control and coordination of these activities, and competitive strategy in multinational enterprises (1992). The authors used cross-functional definitions (that is, strategy, finance, marketing, operations management, and so on) for these four organizational variables.

Their work also proposed a way to operationalize the two variables. For MA, they suggested that a measure of MA at the company level can be obtained by calculating the weighted product of the number of countries where the firm operates in combination with 'the degree of political risk and cultural distance'. For MV, a similar measurement to MA can be calculated using some kind of weighting scheme (sales, profits, and so on) in combination with changes in the real exchange rate.

4.2 Conceptual framework

This work follows these lines of research and specifically attempts to make contributions in the following areas, by:

a. *Looking at companies' operations in emerging markets*. Most of the earlier works have focused on the US and more recent studies have presented evidence from different developed countries that questions the weak relation found in the US; however, there are few studies on MNEs from developed companies with operations in emerging markets (see, for example, Choi and Kim, 2003). This is relevant since Bodnar and Gebhardt (1999) and Bodnar et al. (2003) found that the different characteristics of the countries can influence the degree of FX exposure experienced by companies in the attitudes to FX risk, the objectives of risk management, and positions involve investments in brand development or other intangible assets; (iv) loans in local currencies may affect the performance and the profitability of companies trading with these currencies due to higher rates of interest in emerging economies' currencies than those in currencies from developed countries; (v) loans, especially large ones, in local currencies are not always available; (vi) the volatility of emerging countries' currencies makes it riskier to borrow long-term as companies could face a maturity mismatch; and (vii) companies borrowing in strong currencies could suffer a currency mismatch paying the capital and services of the loan with revenues in a devalued currency. In other words, the traditional tools and techniques widely used by companies in developed countries may be less efficient in the protection of firm's value in emerging markets.

b. *Taking a broader perspective; not only from the finance position, but also including marketing, operations management, and strategic planning in the analysis.* The broader perspective idea builds upon previous studies that have tried to understand the relationship between changes in the value of currencies and market returns by studying other factors that can affect the FX exposure, such as, for example, the firms' attitude to risk (Faff & Marshall, 2005). This broader, or holistic, approach can also be seen as a step forward from previous works that have analysed the finance managers' attitude towards FX exposure (Allayannis & Ofek, 2001; Faff & Marshall, 2005; Hakkarainen et al., 1998; Joseph & Hewins, 1997; Marshall, 2000; Martin et al., 1999; Pantzalis et al., 2001) by including the views from other functional areas within the company. This holistic approach follows the work from Aggarwal and Soenen (1989), who concluded that firms may make decisions in their different functional areas 'to protect against losses in value related to long-term changes in exchange rate' in their study of MNEs in the US. This work attempts to provide empirical evidence of MNEs from developed countries operating in emerging markets using this holistic approach.

c. *Including the study of qualitative data in addition to the analysis of quantitative data.* The use of qualitative data, which has been suggested by Jones and Khanna (2006), along with other rigorous methods in addition to quantitative information for future studies in International Business, was deemed necessary in order to have a broad view of FX from within the organization so the holistic approach can be applied. And also to avoid the net impact effect of the market-based model explained in section 3.4. The inclusion of qualitative information also marks a difference with previous studies as most of them gathered data through mail surveys (Faff & Marshall, 2005; Marshall, 2000) or from the companies' balance sheets (Choi & Kim, 2003; Miller & Reuer, 1998), but no qualitative and/or mixed approach was attempted. The qualitative data resulted from interviews with senior managers/directors, meetings that also offered the opportunity to discuss the FX exposure issue in great detail with the persons responsible for making the decisions.

4.3 Key themes identified in the literature

Using the framework previously defined and building upon the works mentioned in the sections above, it is possible to identify key themes that are recurrent in the literature about the effects of exchange rate variations in the four management areas of finance, marketing, operations management, and strategic planning (discussed in Chapter 3). These key themes will be the foundations of this study and can be seen in Figure 4.2.

4.4 Objectives and research propositions

This section presents the main argument of this work. It is based on the objectives developed within the conceptual framework described in section 4.2, and the key themes presented in Figure 4.2.

The first objective is to study the movements in the exchange rate's impact on companies operating in emerging markets from a broad perspective. This first objective embraces the main proposition of this work, that a holistic approach to hedging (including the different functional areas, mainly finance, marketing, operations management, and strategic planning) against unexpected variations in the exchange rate is expected to contribute to reducing the impact that these variations have on the value of companies with foreign investments in emerging markets. Within this framework, the analysis will study the relation (if any) between a set of strategies and decisions derived from the key themes listed in Figure 4.2 (referred to as the 'holistic approach') and a foreign exchange (or MV) exposure coefficient. This study is aimed at understanding the relative importance of these strategies when hedging against MV (this process will be explained in more detail in sections 5.5, 5.6, and 5.6.1).

The second objective of this work is the development of a tool that will help companies to improve the effectiveness of their hedging activities in emerging markets. This framework will be based on previous works, the information obtained from the study described above, as well as from the qualitative data gathered from the companies participating in the research (more details will be shown in sections 5.5, 5.6 and 5.6.2).

- Measurement and assessment of economic/operating exposure difficulty (Lees & Mauer, 2002; Martin & Mauer, 2003)
- Stage of the planning process when economic exposure is incorporated (Miller & Reuer, 1998)
- Investments abroad/multinational production networks/geographic diversification as hedging tools (Bodnar et al., 1998; Chow et al., 1997a, 1997b; George & Schroth, 1991; Jacque, 1981; Jorion, 1990; Lessard & Lightstone, 1986; Martin et al., 1999; Martin & Mauer, 2003; Pantzalis et al., 2001; Pringle, 1995)
- Ownership structure policy for foreign investments/reasons to decide investments overseas (Kennedy, 1984)
- Relation (if any) between geographic diversification and degree of exposure (Allayannis & Ofek, 2001; Chow et al., 1997a; Hodder, 1982; Martin & Mauer, 2003; Pringle & Connolly, 1993)
- Strategies of competing firms/Intercountry rivalry in industry (Hodder, 1982; Marston, 2001; Miller & Reuer, 1998; Porter, 1990; Pringle, 1995; Shapiro, 1975; von Ungerm-Sternberg & von Weizssacker, 1990)
- Degree of product differentiation and price elasticity of customer demand (Porter, 1990; Sundaram & Black, 1992; Sundaram & Mishra, 1991)
- Development of formal policies against foreign exchange exposure (Hakkarainen et al., 1998)
- Relation among the development of formal policies with the time since companies started their internationalization process with the intended degree of hedging and with the companies' exposure level (Hakkarainen et al., 1998)
- Participation of finance, marketing, operations management, and strategic planning when making decisions about hedging against foreign exchange risk (Lees & Mauer, 2002; Martin & Mauer, 2003)
- Generation of relevant information within the company, and relation between the different units responsible for generating this information (Lees & Mauer, 2002)
- Centralization/decentralization of decision-making and implementation of hedging activities (Sundaram & Black, 1992)
- Relative use of financial hedging tools/effectiveness of these tools against foreign exchange exposure is unclear (Chow, et al., 1997a, 1997b; Pringle, 1991; Pringle & Connolly, 1993)

Figure 4.2 Key themes

4.5 Conclusion

This chapter has presented the conceptual framework of this work. Previous chapters have described how foreign exchange risk may have an impact upon companies' value using four main management areas. This wider, holistic approach is a difference from mainstream research on foreign exchange exposure which has focused principally on the financial side. The broader approach was developed further in this chapter. Chapter 5 will show how the analysis was undertaken.

5
How the Analysis Was Carried Out

5.1 Introduction

The present chapter applies the concepts described at the end of this volume in Appendix 1 to the specific situation of this work. For clarity, the text will follow the same structure as in the appendix, use the same concepts, and attempt to link them with the particular aspects of this study.

5.2 Research philosophy

Considering what has been presented in previous chapters, the research design assumed that 'reality is external and objective' and that 'knowledge is only of significance if it is based on observations of this external reality' (Easterby-Smith et al., 2002). These assumptions were based upon the fact that the researcher took the position of an external and objective observer of facts, events, decisions, strategies, lessons, and so on, experienced by companies during the period and in the region under analysis, as well as how they were affected by changes in the environment. Other reasons supporting these ontological and epistemological assumptions are: (i) the observer was independent; (ii) the companies' decisions were mainly the result of formal/informal internal processes; (iii) the explanations attempt to demonstrate relationships or patterns among the variables selected for the study; (iv) the research progressed through proposals and deductions; (v) the design first operationalized and then measured the concepts; (vi) the units of analysis were defined in advanced; and

(vii) the main findings are based on statistical analysis (Easterby-Smith et al., 2002).

5.3 Research design

Our research was carried out through the use of a survey. The choice of this design was based on the fact that one of the objectives of the project was to portray an accurate profile (Robson, 2002) and to try to establish patterns or relationships (Easterby-Smith et al., 2002). The project also involved the study of second-hand information such as companies' public documents and reports from international organizations (World Bank, World Trade Organization, Economic Commission for Latin America and the Caribbean, etc.), Datastream International, among other reliable sources. More details of the data collection process will be presented in section 5.5.

5.4 Sample

As mentioned in Chapter 4, this research work focuses on investments from Triad countries (in this instance the EU) in emerging markets (the Mercosur and Chile). This Europe-wide sample contrasts this work very strongly with many of the previous studies which have analysed the US and/or referred to single countries; the same applies for the destination of the investments, as research in this field on emerging markets has been scarce.

The Mercosur countries (Argentina, Brazil, Paraguay, and Uruguay) and Chile are included in the list of 64 emerging economies mentioned in Chapter 2 (section 2.8) and have been studied using the three perspectives presented before (also section 2.8, sub-sections a, b, and c), transaction costs economics (Aulakh et al., 2000; Khanna & Palepu, 2000), institutional theory (Khanna & Palepu, 2000; Suarez & Oliva, 2002), and the resource-based view of the firm (Guillén, 2000). However, these studies did not focus on the impact that variations in the value of the region's currencies had on foreign companies operating in these countries.

It is also important to highlight that the European investments in South America (specifically in the Mercosur countries) present a unique setting to carry out this study. On the one hand, European multinational companies became the largest foreign investor in the region in 1997 (and still hold the top position). These investments were made within a positive relation between the European Union and the Mercosur and Chile. In this sense, the EU recognises that the

> Mercosur and Chile are a growing pole of attraction for the European Union, not only because of the size of the markets (210 million inhabitants), but also because of their growth prospects, which will continue to cause European exports to rise. What is more, the fall in demand for imports on the Asian markets and low demand in the former Eastern-bloc countries have served only to increase the attractiveness of Mercosur and Chile.

The EU adds that the 'establishment of NAFTA illustrates the significant risks which the creation of a free trade area of the Americas (FTAA) ... could entail if not preceded by a free trade agreement between the EU and Mercosur and Chile' (European Commission, 2004). Examples of this good relationship can be seen in the fact that the EU and Chile signed a free trade agreement in 2002; and that, since 1998, the EU and the Mercosur have been negotiating an official free trade agreement. In addition, Latin America has also been one of the top recipients of FDI throughout the twentieth century, meaning that the region is not unfamiliar with hosting MNCs.

On the other hand, over the course of the past 15 years the region has suffered many currency crises – for example, the Tequila crisis (Mexico 1994), the Brazilian devaluation at the beginning of 1999, and the political, economic, financial, and social crisis in Argentina in 2001 (during this period there were also crises in Ecuador, Bolivia, Paraguay, Uruguay, Colombia, and Venezuela; there were also contagion effects in Chile and Costa Rica, generally considered the more stable countries in the region). The time frame for the analysis included the period of economic, political, and financial crises (1998–2001) and their aftermath (2001–2006). Figure 5.1 shows the FDI stock in Latin America by the end of 2003.

The importance of Latin America for European companies can be seen not only in the funds invested in the region (more than US$150,000 million), but also in the sales coming from the region. Table 5.1 shows the largest European companies with operations in South America.

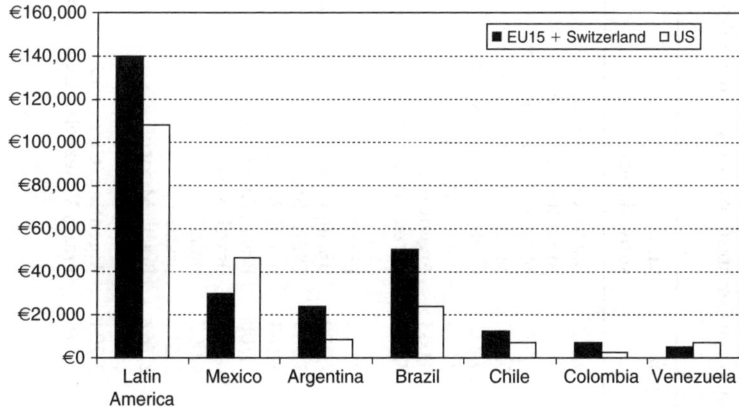

Figure 5.1 Latin America FDI flows by source, end of 2003 (millions of euros)
Source: IADB (2006).

Within this framework, the companies in the sample fulfilled the following requirements:

- Have their headquarters and origins in the European Economic Area (EU-27, Iceland, Liechtenstein, and Norway) + Switzerland,
- Have foreign investments in the emerging countries under study, and
- Sales from these investments should reach at least 5 per cent of their total turnover in 2004 (to be sure that these investments have an impact on the companies' income statement, where 5 per cent represents the estimated share of Latin America in the world's economy) (ECLAC, 2006b).

Our analysis involved the use of information and reports from the stock markets in the different European countries, along with analysis from the member states' embassies and studies from the European Union's offices in Latin American countries. The results showed that around 120 companies can be included in the population. The list can be seen in Appendix 2 at the end of the volume. The analysis of this appendix shows that only a few Spanish companies represented near 50 per cent of the total European investments in the region and,

Table 5.1 Top 50 non-financial European corporations operating in Latin America and the Caribbean by consolidated sales, 2005 (millions of US dollars)

2005	2004	Firm	Country	Sector	Sales	Main subsidiaries
1	3	Telefónica	Spain	Telecommunications	19,425	Brazil, Chile, Peru, Argentina, Mexico
4	4	DaimlerChrysler	Germany	Automotive	15,971	Mexico, Brazil,Argentina
5	5	Volkswagen	Germany	Automotive	15,680	Mexico, Brazil, Argentina
7	7	Endesa	Spain	Electricity	10,252	Chile, Brazil, Argentina
8	9	Telecom Italia	Italy	Telecommunications	9,904	Brazil, Argentina
8	8	Repsol-YPF	Spain	Oil/Gas	8,033	Argentina, Peru
10	14	Royal Dutch/Shell	Netherlands/UK	Oil/Gas	8,033	Brazil, Argentina
11	24	Arcelor	Luxembourg	Steel	7,747	Brazil
12	13	Carrefour	France	Commerce	7,229	Brazil, Colombia, Argentina
14	21	BHP Billiton PLC	Australia/UK	Mining	5,989	Chile, Brazil, Peru
19	20	Nestlé	Switzerland	Food	5,183	Brazil, Mexico
20	30	Fiat Auto	Italy	Motor Vehicle	4,708	Brazil, Argentina
22	26	Siemens	Germany	Electronics	4,210	Brazil, Mexico
23	29	Iberdrola SA	Spain	Electricity	4,007	Brazil
25	34	Portugal Telecom	Portugal	Telecommunications	3,611	Brazil
28	28	Bayer	Germany	Petrochemical/ Chemicals	2,762	Brazil, Mexico
29	50	BP Amoco	UK	Petroleum/Gas	2,704	Argentina, Colombia
30	32	British American Tobacco	UK	Tobacco	2,676	Brazil, Venezuela, Argentina

31	31	Anglo American Plc	UK	Mining	2,636	Chile
33		Renault	France	Motor vehicle	2,298	Brazil, Colombia, Argentina
34	48	Electricité de France	France	Electricity	2,087	Brazil
36	47	Sonae SGPS	Portugal	Commerce	1,978	Brazil
38	15	Unilever	Netherlands/UK	Agro-industry	1,851	Mexico, Argentina
41		Robert Bosch Gmbh	Germany	Motor vehicle parts	1,715	Brazil
42	46	BASF	Germany	Petrochemical/ Chemical	1,651	Brazil
44		Mittal Steel Co.	Netherlands	Steel	1,551	Mexico
45		Volvo	Sweden	Motor vehicle	1,505	Brazil
48		Rhodia	France	Petrochemical/ Chemical	1,482	Brazil
50		Makro	Netherlands	Commerce	1,441	Brazil
				Total	159,933	

Source: ECLAC (2006a) on the basis of information provided by the Special Studies and Projects Department of *Américaeconomía* magazine, Santiago, Chile, 2006.

This table was produced by aggregating the sales of the subsidiaries of each transnational corporation operating in the region, on the basis of primary information on the sales of the largest companies. In cases where the subsidiary is owned by two or more transnational corporations, its sales are distributed among them according to the percentage ownership of each parent company. This is the case with: Vivo (Brazil), which belongs to Telefónica of Spain and Portugal Telecom; Doña Inés de Collahuasi mining company (Chile), owned by AngloAmerican (United Kingdom) and Falconbridge (Canada/United Kingdom); and the mining company Antamina (Peru), owned by BHP Billiton (Australia/United Kingdom) and Falconbridge (this last example is not included in the list). In terms of the subsidiaries in the region, the table mentions only those for which sales information was available, which means that the list does not necessarily include all subsidiaries of each transnational corporation.

therefore, it was evident that they should have a prominent place (a detailed list of the Spanish investments can be seen in Table 5.2).

44 European companies agreed to participate in the study, a sample that represents over 50 per cent of the money invested in the region. The list of these companies (parent, subsidiary, and origin) can be found in Table 5.3. The sample includes companies from different origins as well as from different industries.

5.5 Data collection

As mentioned earlier, data collection was based mainly on interviews containing structured and open-ended questions with senior managers, directors, or members of the board of the companies participating in the study. These were supplemented by the collection of second-hand information from the companies, national governments, and multinational organizations.

The interviews were carried out in Spain, the UK, Argentina, and Chile, as well as a few by telephone (in the US, France, and Italy). The structure of the interviews as well as the required information was based on the "key themes" identified in the analysis of the literature (section 4.3, Figure 4.2). These key themes can be revisited in Figure 5.2 and their links with the aims and variables of this study will be analysed in more detail in later sections (mainly 5.6.1).

The interviews followed a logical structure: introduction, warm-up, main body, cool-off, and closure; they were tape-recorded when permission from the interviewee was granted (in only one case was this permission not obtained), and they took an average of 60 minutes. The first version of the interview was developed and pilot tested in English, then translated into Spanish (pilot tested again), and finally re-translated back into English. This back-translation was carried out by two independent translators on top of the version produced by the researcher. Finally, the three versions were compared and a new final version was created and also pilot tested.

5.6 Data analysis

The analysis of the data gathered through the process described above was carried out from two different perspectives: (i) quantitative analysis for both the data collected with the structured questions of the

Table 5.2 Cumulative net investment by some Spanish firms in Latin America, 2003

Company	€	%	Cumul.	Company	€	%	Cumul.	Company	€	%	Cumul.
Telefónica	32,650	34.20	34.20	Corp. Mapfre	454	0.48	96.57	FCC	100	0.10	99.57
Repsol YPF	20,858	21.85	56.05	Abertis	430	0.45	97.02	REE	88	0.09	99.66
G. Santander	16,433	17.21	73.27	Dragados	344	0.36	97.38	Acciona	70	0.07	99.73
Telef. Móviles	5,330	5.58	78.85	Ferrovial	326	0.34	97.73	Ebro Puleva	67	0.07	99.80
BBVA	5,143	5.39	84.24	OHL	300	0.31	98.04	Amper	64	0.07	99.87
Endesa	3,117	3.27	87.50	NH Hoteles	230	0.24	98.28	Viscofán	53	0.06	99.92
Iberdrola	2,800	2.93	90.43	Terra Lycos	227	0.24	98.52	Abengoa	25	0.03	99.95
Unión Fenosa	2,493	2.61	93.05	Prosegur	225	0.24	98.75	Aldeasa	20	0.02	99.97
Gas Natural	860	0.90	93.95	Inditex	170	0.18	98.93	Mecalux	10	0.01	99.98
AgBar	561	0.59	94.53	Prisa	152	0.16	99.09	Iberia	10	0.01	99.99
Altadis	508	0.53	95.07	Sacyr Valleh.	136	0.14	99.23	Amdeus	5	0.01	100.0
Sol Meliá	500	0.52	95.59	TPI	111	0.12	99.35	Indra	3	0.00	100.0
Arcelor	484	0.51	96.10	ACS	105	0.11	99.46	**Total**	**95,462**		

Source: Adapted from Arahuetes and Casilda (2004).

Table 5.3 Companies participating in the study

Subsidiary	Origin	Parent Company
Endesa	Spain	Endesa
Repsol YPF	Spain	Repsol YPF
Banco Bilbao Vizcaya Argentaria (BBVA)	Spain	Banco Bilbao Vizcaya Argentaria
Grupo Santander	Spain	Grupo Santander
Iberdrola	Spain	Iberdrola
Telefónica	Spain	Telefonica
Gas Natural	Spain	Gas Natural
Reed Exhibitions	UK	Reed Exhibitions
Lloyds TSB	UK	Lloyds TSB
Marconi	UK	Marconi
Halcrow	UK	Halcrow
Halcrow	UK	Halcrow
Porsche	Germany	Porsche
France Telecom	France	France Telecom
Mallarsa	Italy	Grupo RTR
OSM	France	Saur
Distrocuyo	France	Electricite de France
Ecogas	Germany	E-on
NH Cordillera	Spain	NH Hoteles
Navarro Correas	UK	Diageo
Bodegas Chandon	France	LVMH
Hinisa/Hidisa	France	Electricite de France
Monteviejo	Netherlands	Chateau Montviel
O. Fournier	Spain	O. Fournier
Bodegas Norton	Austria	Swarovski
Cardif	France	Banque Nationale Paris
Puratos	Belgium	Puratos
Royal & SunAlliance	UK	Royal & SunAlliance
Wartsila	Finland	Wartsila
Banco Santander Santiago	Spain	Grupo Santander
Man Ferrostaal	Germany	Man Ferrostaal
Movistar	Spain	Movistar (Telefonica Moviles)
Sodexho Pass	France	Sodexho Pass
Citroen Chile	France	PSA Peugeot Citroën
Bayer	Germany	Bayer
ABB	Sweden	ABB
Pan American Energy	UK	British Petroleum
Royal & SunAlliance	UK	Royal & SunAlliance
Edenor	France	Electricite de France
Ipsos Latin America	France	Ipsos
Lanxess	Germany	Lanxess
Nobleza Piccardo	UK	British American Tobacco
Aerolineas Argentinas	Spain	Grupo Marsans
Rayen Cura	France	Saint Gobain

- Measurement and assessment of economic/operating exposure difficulty
- Stage of the planning process when economic exposure is incorporated
- Investments abroad/multinational production networks/geographic diversification as hedging tools
- Ownership structure policy for foreign investments/reasons to decide investments overseas
- Relation (if any) between geographical diversification and degree of exposure
- Strategies of competing firms/intercountry rivalry in industry
- Degree of product differentiation and the price elasticity of customer demand
- Development of formal policies against foreign exchange exposure
- Relation among the development of formal policies with the time since companies started their internationalization process with the intended degree of hedging and with the companies' exposure level
- Participation of finance, marketing, operations management, and strategic planning when making decisions about hedging against foreign exchange risk
- Generation of relevant information within the company, and relation between the different units responsible for generating this information
- Centralization/decentralization of decision-making and the implementation of hedging activities
- Relative use of financial hedging tools

Figure 5.2 Key themes revisited

interview and the second-hand information; and (ii) qualitative analysis for the open-ended questions. Following this, the quantitative and qualitative analyses were combined.

5.6.1 Quantitative analysis

The quantitative analysis was carried out in a similar way to that adopted in previous papers (see, inter alia, Allayannis & Ofek, 2001; Choi & Kim, 2003; Chow & Chen, 1998; Faff & Marshall, 2005; Guay, 1999) where a coefficient of the foreign exchange exposure of the sampled companies is calculated through a first-stage time series regression of the companies' stock returns on market and foreign exchange returns. In this context, foreign exchange risk was defined as changes in the value of the firm as a consequence of changes in the value of the currency. However, there is a difference in the use of real exchange rates – rather than the nominal exchange rates used by most of those papers. This is because 'the random walk and the market efficiency hypotheses might make both nominal and real exchange rates acceptable for advanced industrialised countries' but for emerging economies like the ones under study the 'same degree of market efficiency cannot be expected' (Choi & Kim, 2003). This coefficient was calculated using contemporaneous exchange rate as the evidence between contemporaneous and lagged is mixed and there is no theory to state what length of lag is appropriate. The equation used can be seen below:

$$R_{it} = \alpha + \beta_m R_{mt} + \beta_{fx} R_{fxt} + \varepsilon_{it} \qquad (2)$$

where R_{it} is the return of company i in period t, R_{mt} is the return for the market index in period t, and R_{fxt} is the return on real exchange rate in period t.

Then, the foreign exchange rate risk exposure coefficients were included in a second-stage cross-sectional regression on the variables derived from the survey responses using the following formula:

$$\begin{aligned}\beta_{fx,i} = {} & a + \theta_1 INDUSTRY_i + \theta_2 CURRENCIES_i + \theta_3 ORIGIN_i \\ & + \theta_4 OWNERSHIP_i + \theta_5 NEXTINVEST_i + \theta_6 IHORIZON_i \\ & + \theta_7 STAGE2_i + \theta_8 BENCHMARK2_i + \theta_9 FXPOLICY2_i \\ & + \theta_{10} AREAS2_i + \theta_{11} AREAS3_i + \theta_{12} AUTDECISION2_i \\ & + \theta_{13} AUTDECISION3_i + \theta_{14} AUTIMPLEMENT2_i \\ & + \theta_{15} AUTIMPLEMENT3_i + \theta_{16} ERRISK_i + \theta_{17} HTUSE_i \\ & + \theta_{18} COUNTRIES_i + \varepsilon_i \qquad (3)\end{aligned}$$

where $\beta_{fx,}$ is the value of the estimated exposure coefficient. The definitions of the variables and their links with the questions in the survey can be seen below:

INDUSTRY: categorical variable, indicating the industry in which the company is operating. 1 = Telecommunications, 2 = Petroleum and chemicals, 3 = Power generation and distribution, 4 = Gas distribution, 5 = Commercial banks and insurance, 6 = Professional services, 7 = Car manufacturers, 8 = Hotels, 9 = Manufacture and the commercialization of branded products, 10 = Wine production, 11 = Food production, 12 = Machinery manufacturer, 13 = Drugs and medicines, 14 = Tobacco, 15 = Airlines, 16 = Water distribution, 17 = Glass production. This variable is expected to have a negative relation as the industries in the sample have a tradition of international operations.

CURRENCIES: this is a categorical variable, indicating the number of currencies involved in the cash flow of the company on top of the home currency, where 1 = 1–5 currencies, 2 = 6–10 currencies, 3 = 11–15 currencies, and 4 = more than 16 currencies. This represents a proxy for 'Relation between geographic diversification and degree of exposure' (Figure 4.2) which is expected to have a positive relation with the magnitude of foreign exchange rate exposure (although it is possible that this positive relation could become negative as the number of countries grows, the exposure could be offset by operating with multiple currencies in different countries).

ORIGIN: is a nominal variable, indicating the country of origin of the company. 1 = Austria, 2 = Belgium, 3 = Finland, 4 = France, 5 = Germany, 6 = Italy, 7 = Netherlands, 8 = Spain, 9 = Sweden, 10 = the UK. This variable is expected to have a negative relation as the countries' economies in the sample have a relatively long tradition in international ventures (Hakkarainen et al., 1998).

OWNERSHIP: is a categorical variable, which gives the answers to the question 'In terms of ownership structure of foreign investments, which of the following describes your company's policy?' where 1 = 100 per cent ownership, 2 = majority control, 3 = joint venture 50/50, 4 = minority stake, 5 = no specific policy. A proxy for 'Ownership structure policy for foreign investments/reasons to decide investments overseas' (Figure 4.2) and the relationship with the size of the exposure is expected to be negative as the majority control held by parents gives subsidiaries the opportunity to base their operations on the parents' advantages (management, knowledge, proprietary assets, technology, access to markets, brands, etc.) and, as a consequence, hedge their cash flows (Kennedy, 1984).

NEXTINVEST: is a categorical variable, which gives the answers to the question 'Where is your company more likely to make the next long-term investment?' where 1 = in a country using the same currency as where the company's headquarters is located, 2 = in a country using the same currency as the majority of the income of the company, 3 = in a country using a currency like the US dollar, euro, pound, or Yen, 4 = the most important factors are the business prospects, not the currency. Within 'Investments abroad/multinational production networks/geographic diversification as hedging tools' (Figure 4.2), 1, 2, and 3 are expected to have a negative relation, and 4 a positive relation with the magnitude of the foreign exchange rate exposure.

IHORIZON: is a scale variable, which gives the answers to the question 'In terms of years, what do you mean by "long-term investments"?' where 1 = 1–5, 2 = 6–10, 3 = 11–15, 4 = more than 16. This variable attempts to assess the companies' long-term intentions when investing abroad and also falls within 'Investments abroad/multinational production networks/geographic diversification as hedging tools' (Figure 4.2). Its relationship with the magnitude of the exposure is expected to be negative; the longer the period, the smaller the exposure. This is principally because it is thought that a company with intentions to be present in a certain market overseas for a long time should put in place mechanisms to decrease its exposure to the foreign exchange rate. Twenty years (20) was entered for companies answering something like 'we have invested to stay'.

STAGE: is a dummy variable, which gives the answers to the question 'In which stage does your company take into consideration economic exposure when investing abroad?' where 0 = when the subsidiary is operating (reference group) and 1 = planning stage. A proxy for 'Stage of the planning process when economic exposure is incorporated' (Figure 4.2) where 1 is expected to have a negative relation with the reference group as the company would be thinking on this risk even before the subsidiary is set up abroad (which, as the literature suggests, reduce the exposure).

BENCHMARK: is a dummy variable, which gives the answers to the question 'Once the subsidiaries are operating abroad, does your company study what the competitors do to protect their investments against economic exposure?' where 0 = no (reference group) and 1 = yes. Within the key theme 'Strategies of competing firms/Intercountry rivalry in industry' (Figure 4.2), it is expected to have a negative impact against the reference group when the answer is 1. This is because the effects of changes in the exchange rate can also come from competitors, as their competitiveness can improve (worsen) depending on their cost structures and value chain.

FXPOLICY: is a dummy variable, which gives the answers to the question 'Has your company developed an exchange rate hedging policy?' where 0 = no (reference group) and 1 = yes. This question attempts to be a proxy for the 'Development of formal policies against foreign exchange exposure' (Figure 4.2); the answers with 1 are predicted to have a negative relationship with the reference group as suggested by the literature (in this context, the answers with 0 would have a positive relation).

AREAS2 and *AREAS3*: are dummy variables, which show the answers to the question 'When your company assesses the exchange rate risk, does it include other departments besides finance?' where *AREAS1* (the reference group) = marketing and operations, *AREAS2* = finance-related, and *AREAS3* = finance. This variable is a proxy for 'Participation of finance, marketing, operations management, and strategic planning when making decisions about hedging against foreign exchange risk' (Figure 4.2) where *AREAS2* and *AREAS3* are predicted to have a positive relation in comparison to *AREAS1*.

AUTDECISION2 and *AUTDECISION3*: are dummy variables, which give the answers to the question 'What degrees of freedom do the subsidiaries have in hedging their exchange rate exposure in terms of decision-making?' where *AUTDECISION1* (the reference group) = high, *AUTDECISION2* = middle, *AUTDECISION3* = low. Variable proxy for 'Centralization/decentralization of decision-making and implementation of hedging activities' (Figure 4.2) and, as the literature suggests, *AUTDECISION2* and *AUTDECISION3* are predicted to have a positive relationship with the reference group.

AUTIMPLEMENT2 and *AUTIMPLEMENT3*: are dummy variables, which give the answers to the question 'What degrees of freedom do the subsidiaries have in hedging their exchange rate exposure in terms of implementation?' where *AUTIMPLEMENT1* (the reference group) = high, *AUTIMPLEMENT2* = middle, *AUTIMPLEMENT3* = low. Another variable proxy for 'Centralization/decentralization of decision-making and implementation of hedging activities' (Figure 4.2); as the literature suggests, *AUTIMPLEMENT2* and *AUTIMPLEMENT3* are predicted to have a positive relationship with the reference group.

ERRISK: is a categorical variable, which gives the answers to the question 'In terms of percentage, from what variation level will you start considering exchange rate as a risk?' where 1 = 1–5, 2 = 6–10,

3 = 11–15, 4 = more than 16. This question attempted to measure the level of risk that companies accept to take and is expected to have a positive relationship with the exposure to the foreign exchange rate; i.e., the larger the level that the company considers exchange rate as a risk, the larger the magnitude of the exposure.

HTUSE: is a categorical variable, which represents the relative use of hedging tools in emerging markets, where 0 = not used, 1 = very frequently, 2 = frequently, 3 = sometimes, 4 = not frequently, and 5 = infrequently. This question falls within the 'Relative use of financial hedging tools' key theme (Figure 4.2) where 0, 5, 4, and 3 are expected to have a positive relation and 1 and 2 a negative relationship with the size of the exposure.

COUNTRIES: this is a categorical variable, which shows the number of countries where the company is operating, where 1 = 1–5, 2 = 6–10, 3 = 11–15, and 4 = over 16. This represents a proxy for 'Relation between geographic diversification and degree of exposure' (Figure 4.2) which is expected to have a positive relation with the magnitude of foreign exchange rate exposure (although it is possible that this positive relation could become negative as the number of countries grows, the exposure could be offset by operating with multiple currencies in different countries).

This model includes most of the key themes listed in '*Figure 4.2* Key themes' using the data collected in the interviews. It is possible to see that the focus of some question/variables was the attitude of the companies when deciding investments abroad and managing risk (an approach shared by other works – for example, Faff & Marshall, 2005). This is because the measurement of the exposure using either the cash flow-based or market-based models shows net impacts and the aim of this model was to see the impact (if any) of the companies' decisions on the exposure. For this reason, the model was built thinking on ex ante strategies/decisions rather than on ex post decisions (such as the use of hedging tools; in fact, the *HTUSE* variable was included to reflect the effects of hedging tools in the exposure). In addition, this is also linked with the main argument of this work; to take a 'holistic approach' to hedging in emerging markets the decisions [variables] from the different management areas should be considered. This approach contrasts with the ex post approach of using financial tools to hedge flows in different currencies (the case in most developed countries).

Variables *STAGE1*, *BENCHMARK1*, *FXPOLICY1*, *AREAS1*, *AUTDECISION1*, and *AUTIMPLEMENT1* were not included in the model to avoid the dummy variable trap as they represent the reference group.[1] The answers obtained under the remaining key themes listed in Figure 4.2 (Measurement and assessment of economic/operating exposure difficulty, Degree of product differentiation and price elasticity of customer demand, Relation among the development of formal policies with the time since companies started their internationalization process with the intended degree of hedging and with the companies' exposure level, Generation of relevant information within the company, and Relation between the different units responsible for generating this information) were not included in this regression as the information was not possible to be standardized or because many interviewees did not provide a response. Some of these points will be included in the qualitative analysis.

Equation 3 was calculated twice. The regression equation was run (using the simultaneous method) to obtain the relationship between the variables in the model with the aim of using this information to see the relationships or interactions between the decisions and the foreign exchange exposure. Then the regression was run using the stepwise multiple regression in order to obtain the highest statistically significant correlation with the independent variable into the regression analysis. In this second case, the aim was to see which of the variables has the highest impact on the exposure as well as to rank them according to their effects.

The cross-sectional regression was then re-run twice to check the robustness of the model using alternative definitions of foreign exchange rate risk. First, the absolute value of the t-statistics of the exposure estimate, $|t|$, was used as dependent variable because it shows the precision with which the foreign exchange rate risk is estimated (Faff & Marshall, 2005). Second, the dependent variable used was the absolute value of the estimated exposure coefficient, $|\beta_{fx}|$. The absolute values are used as it is argued that the sign of the exposure coefficient attempts to show the direction of the risk exposure, for example, importer versus exporter, and, in this case, what is relevant is the magnitude of the risk exposure, not the direction (Choi & Prasad, 1995; Faff & Marshall, 2005). Selected responses from the structured questions used in this analysis can be seen in Appendix 3 at the end of the volume.

5.6.2 Qualitative analysis

As explained in Appendix 1 (section A1.7.2), the foundation of a qualitative analysis is the effective coding of the collected data. In this study, the first 'natural' coding was done by the structured questions in the survey. These questions offered the main framework for the interviews and provided important amounts of rich data that complemented the quantitative answers. On average, the 'quantitative part' of the interviews represented around 40 per cent. For the remaining 60 per cent of the time the main objective of the interviews was to collect 'qualitative' data on the decisions, actions, strategies, experiences, etc., of the companies in their ventures in South America.

The qualitative data were analysed and coded using the first two approaches outlined in Glaser and Strauss (1967).[2] First, the data (mainly from the structured questions) was converted to quantifiable form and used in Equation 22; secondly, the qualitative data were reviewed to redesign and reintegrate the initial framework. A combination (to a certain extent) of the two approaches was attempted, although the third approach was not applied because theoretical sampling[3] was not used. The objective was to base the analysis on the analytical side of the first approach and the possibility of developing new categories, hypotheses, and interrelated hypotheses of the second. In this context, the group of the top Spanish investors was studied in great detail.

The unit of analysis for the qualitative study was the different incidents (which varied from a single phrase or sentence, to an entire comment consisting of two or three sentences (Titscher et al., 2000)) reported by the participants. These incidents were sorted under the categories that were emerging as the review of the data went on. During this continuous process, the categories and their incidents were compared which generated properties that then were integrated with the categories. As the process of comparison started to produce fewer new results, the next step saw the consolidation of the categories and their properties. Finally, the conclusions were summarized and combined with the quantitative analysis.

Throughout the text there has been discussion of the issue of external validity. The approach chosen to assure this validity was the inclusion of detailed explanations of the processes with the aim of providing a framework for potential comparisons (Merrian, 1998). In this context, three strategies were applied and explained throughout

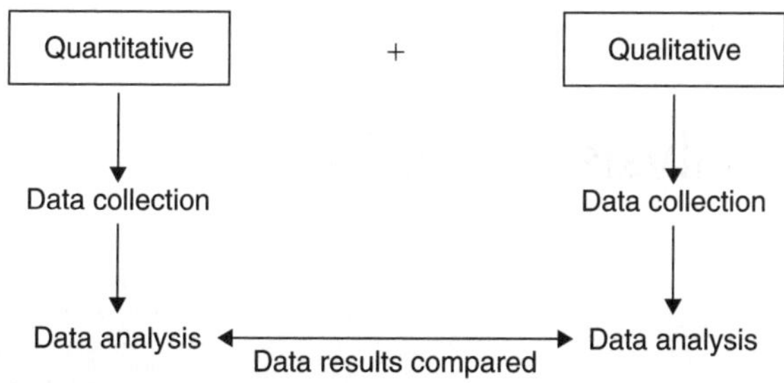

Figure 5.3 Concurrent triangulation strategy
Source: Creswell (2003).

this work: (i) the provision of detailed explanations of the aim of the study, the researcher's position, the participants' interests, and the context in which the data was collected; (ii) the triangulation or use of multiple methods for collecting data to strengthen the reliability and the internal validity; and (iii) the data gathering and its analysis was 'reported in detail in order to provide a clear and accurate picture of the methods used in this study' (Creswell, 2003).

5.6.3 Mixed method

Concurrent triangulation was the strategy selected for the combined quantitative and qualitative analyses. This is a widely-used method for research works that need to complement, 'confirm, cross-validate, or corroborate findings within a single study' (Creswell, 2003). In this case, the integration took place during the interpretation phase to analyse the relation, difference, and similitude between the qualitative and quantitative parts. The validity and reliability was provided by the methodologies applied during the analyses phases (explained in sections 5.6.1 and 5.6.2). Figure 5.3 presents this strategy.

5.7 Conclusion

This chapter has discussed how the analysis undertaken in this study was carried out. In addition, the mixed method used for the study of quantitative and qualitative data together was explained at the end. The next chapter will show the results of these analyses.

6
The Analysis of the Data

6.1 Introduction

This chapter will present the results of the analysis of the data described in sections 5.6.1, 5.6.2, and 5.6.3 of the previous chapter. It will first show the results from the quantitative analysis; then it will look at the outcome from the qualitative analysis; finally, it will detail the results of the application of both methods.

6.2 Quantitative analysis: results

The first step of this quantitative analysis was the calculation of a coefficient of foreign exchange exposure using Equation 2. This coefficient attempts to show the sensitivity of the companies' value to changes in the exchange rate of the countries under study using the return on market indices[1] as statistical control. The real exchange rate for Argentina, Brazil and Chile was used as these countries have been recipients of the largest investments from European companies in South America (Figure 5.1).[2]

Equity return data and market indexes were sourced from Datastream International, and exchange rate information from Banco Central de Chile (for Chile), Banco Central de la República Argentina (for Argentina), and Ipeadata for Brazil.[3] The regression equation was run only for 32 companies, as the data for the remaining 12 were not reliable, not available, the subsidiary was sold after the start of the research project, or because the company was listed only a short time before the study and therefore did not cover the period under analysis. Monthly data from 1 January 1998 to 1 June 2006 was used[4] and the calculations were carried out using SPSS 12.0 for Windows. The outcome of these calculations can be seen in Table 6.1, which shows the estimates for market risk and foreign exchange exposure.

Table 6.1 Estimates for market risk and foreign exchange exposure, t statistics in italics

	β_m	β_{fx}		β_m	β_{fx}
Co 1	0.11	–0.43	Co 24	0.01	0.24
t	*7.72*	*–2.95*	*t*	*14.10*	*6.39*
Co 2	0.17	10.46	Co 25	0.00	0.08
t	*4.52*	*8.61*	*t*	*6.80*	*2.55*
Co 3	0.01	–0.11	Co 26	0.13	28.89
t	*14.30*	*–6.37*	*t*	*3.20*	*7.51*
Co 4	0.00	–0.01	Co 27		
t	*14.22*	*–1.96*	*t*		
Co 5	0.01	0.32	Co 28	0.00	0.00
t	*9.73*	*10.65*	*t*	*5.82*	*0.73*
Co 6	0.13	2.90	Co 29		
t	*14.20*	*10.05*	*t*		
Co 7			Co 30	0.06	5.01
t			*t*	*5.73*	*10.61*
Co 8	0.00	0.27	Co 31		
t	*5.46*	*9.63*	*t*		
Co 9	0.04	2.37	Co 32		
t	*2.65*	*5.32*	*t*		
Co 10	0.00	–4.73	Co 33	0.00	–4.73
t	*0.11*	*–9.43*	*t*	*0.11*	*–9.43*
Co 11			Co 34	0.01	–0.08
t			*t*	*0.61*	*–0.19*
Co 12	0.00	0.00	Co 35	0.00	0.04
t	*7.59*	*0.07*	*t*	*12.53*	*4.91*
Co 13	0.00	–0.02	Co 36	0.00	0.07
t	*10.41*	*–1.98*	*t*	*4.68*	*2.79*
Co 14	0.02	–0.48	Co 37		
t	*7.91*	*–5.86*	*t*		
Co 15	0.00	0.02	Co 38	0.00	–0.00
t	*6.26*	*2.16*	*t*	*11.13*	*–0.23*
Co 16	0.00	–0.00	Co 39		
t	*11.13*	*–0.23*	*t*		

(Continued)

Table 6.1 (Continued)

	β_m	β_{fx}		β_m	β_{fx}
Co 17			Co 40	0.00	−0.15
t			*t*	*5.39*	*−5.63*
Co 18			Co 41		
t			*t*		
Co 19	0.00	0.08	Co 42	0.00	0.00
t	*7.88*	*7.69*	*t*	*7.59*	*0.07*
Co 20	0.00	−0.00	Co 43		
t	*7.74*	*−0.05*	*t*		
Co 21	0.01	0.49	Co 44	0.02	−0.04
t	*5.53*	*4.32*	*t*	*21.51*	*−2.24*
Co 22	0.01	−0.36	**Mean**	**0.02**	**1.15**
t	4.69	−1.70	**Min**	**0.00**	**−4.73**
Co 23	0.04	−3.16	**Max**	**0.17**	**28.9**
t	*1.98*	*−5.05*	**Positive**	**32**	**20**

In this figure it is possible to see that the mean market risk (β_m) across the sample is 0.025, with a minimum of 0.001 and a maximum of 0.173. All of the companies have a positive beta estimate, and the vast majority of these positive betas are statistically significant ($|\beta_m/S_b| > t_{n-3;\ 0.975}$). It is also possible to see that the mean foreign exchange risk (β_{fx}) is 1.154, with a minimum of −4.733 and a maximum of 28.89. In this case, the majority of these estimates are statistically significant ($|\beta_{fx}/S_b,| > t_{n-3;\ 0.975}$). This was expected as the companies in the sample have foreign exchange exposure due to their overseas operations. The non-statistically significant estimates as well as the negative ones could be explained by the companies' hedging activities or the offsetting impact of their operations in multiple currencies (Allayannis & Ofek, 2001; Faff & Marshall, 2005). The mean of the absolute value of the foreign exchange exposure (not shown in the figure) is 2.049 (1.183 if the 28.89 entry from Co 26 is not considered). Finally, the mean absolute value of the foreign exchange exposure for the group of the top Spanish investors is 0.025.

The second step was the calculation of the results from the cross-sectional regression shown in Equation 3.[5] The market risk mean (β_m) across this new sample is 0.0150, the mean foreign exchange exposure (β_{fx}) is 0.2004, and the mean of the absolute value of the foreign exchange exposure ($|\beta_m|$) is 0.33. All of the top Spanish investors remain in the sample and the group of companies still accounts for over 50 per cent of the funds invested in the region.

Appendix 4 presents the correlation matrix where we can see the relatively high statistically significant correlations between *INDUSTRY* and *IHORIZON*, *CURRENCIES* and *COUNTRIES*, and, *CURRENCIES* and *HTUSE*. These relatively high correlations are, to a certain extent, expected and possible reasons for them could include: in the first case, because some industries need more time to mature their investments; in the second case, because the higher the number of countries, the higher the number of currencies (especially in Latin America where there is no single currency); and in the third case, because when companies operate in more countries, it is more likely that they will use hedging tools to protect their cash flows. The correlation between *INDUSTRY* and *ERRISK* could be attributed to the fact that different industries operate differently (such as supply chains and retail operations) and as a consequence the fluctuations in the exchange rate affect industries in different ways.

Table 6.2 (Reg 1) shows the results of running Equation 3. It shows that *IHORIZON*, *FXPOLICY2*, and *AUTDECISION2* are clearly significant, and that there is also some role for *INDUSTRY*, *OWNERSHIP*, *STAGE2*, *AREAS2*, and *AUTIMPLEMENT2*. In addition, a stepwise regression also presents that *ORIGIN*, *FXPOLICY2*, and *AUTIMPLEMENT2* explain the greatest and significant proportions of the variance in the dependent variable;[6] Table 6.2 shows the results of the Stepwise regression. In other words, in this sample the raw foreign exchange exposure does not seem to be affected by *CURRENCIES*, *COUNTRIES*, *NEXTINVEST*, *BENCHMARK2*, *AREAS3*, *AUTDECISION3*, *AUTIMPLEMENT3*, *ERRISK*, and *HTUSE*. A possible reason for this (mainly for *NEXTINVEST*, and *ERRISK*) could be that companies in the sample have some experience dealing with operations overseas and do not see problems in investing in places using different currencies or in the relatively high variations in the value of these currencies. This 'experiential' reason could also be applied to *CURRENCIES* and *COUNTRIES*, companies in the sample seem not to be affected because they have been operating in different locations and have learnt how to deal with the problem, or because their operations in different countries/with different currencies offset their exposure. The *HTUSE* case could be explained as many companies said that hedging using

Table 6.2 Cross-sectional regression exploring potential determinants of FX exposure

	Panel A: dependent variable β_{fx}								Panel B: dependent variable $\|t\|$							
	Reg 1		Reg 2		Reg 3		Reg 4		Reg 1		Reg 2		Reg 3		Reg 4	
	β	*t*	β	*t*	β	*t*	β	*t*	β	*t*	β	*t*	β	*t*	β	*t*
a	−5.42	*−1.53*	−1.21	*−2.09*	−0.72	*−1.89*	−0.72	*−3.66*	−1.02	*−0.04*	4.69	*1.37*	5.30	*2.72*	5.30	*5.25*
INDUSTRY	0.07	*1.65*	0.04	*1.33*					0.03	*0.09*	0.05	*0.28*				
CURRENCIES	0.29	*0.70*							*0.99*	0.32						
ORIGIN	0.08	*0.96*	0.16	*3.01*	0.15	*2.66*	0.15	*5.15*	−0.07	*−0.11*	−0.29	*−0.88*	−0.30	*−1.06*	−0.30	*−2.05*
COUNTRIES	0.47	*0.71*							1.05	*0.22*						
OWNERSHIP	−0.19	*−1.36*	−0.27	*−2.08*	−0.28	*−2.10*	−0.28	*−4.06*	−0.83	*−0.79*	−1.03	*−1.37*	−1.06	*−1.54*	−1.06	*−2.97*
IHORIZON	0.28	*2.28*	0.31	*2.90*	0.21	*2.16*	0.21	*4.18*	0.88	*0.96*	1.12	*1.79*	0.99	*2.02*	0.99	*3.91*
STAGE2	−0.46	*−1.48*	−0.32	*−1.18*					0.67	*0.29*	−0.43	*−0.27*				
BENCHMARK2	0.53	*1.29*							−1.18	*−0.39*						
FXPOLICY2	−1.44	*−3.55*	−1.26	*−4.04*	−1.24	*−4.08*	−1.24	*−7.88*	−4.37	*−1.46*	−4.37	*−2.36*	−4.34	*−2.80*	−4.34	*−5.41*
AREAS2	−1.12	*−1.77*	−1.29	*−2.80*	−1.14	*−2.35*	−1.14	*−4.54*	−5.98	*−1.28*	−6.81	*−2.49*	−6.61	*−2.67*	−6.61	*−5.16*
AREAS3	0.83	*1.35*							−0.39	*−0.09*						
AUTDECISION2	1.11	*2.38*	0.68	*1.70*	0.94	*3.13*	0.94	*6.05*	2.35	*0.68*	3.55	*1.51*	3.93	*2.55*	3.93	*4.94*
AUTIMPLEMENT2	1.09	*1.81*	0.51	*1.27*					−1.03	*−0.23*	0.71	*0.30*				
AUTIMPLEMENT3	0.44	*1.31*							−2.08	*−0.84*						
ERRISK	0.32	*0.98*							−0.79	*−0.33*						
HTUSE	−0.15	*−1.34*							0.04	*0.05*						
R^2	0.84		0.70		0.59		0.59		0.54		0.46		0.45		0.45	

[illegible]	[illegible]	[illegible]	[illegible]	[illegible]	−0.33	−1.19	−0.35	−2.30
INDUSTRY	0.04	*1.01*	0.02	*1.00*				
CURRENCIES	0.08	*0.23*						
ORIGIN	0.10	*1.49*	0.13	*3.20*	0.13	*3.08*	0.13	*5.95*
COUNTRIES	0.54	*1.01*						
OWNERSHIP	−0.24	*−2.15*	−0.27	*−2.75*	−0.29	*−2.86*	−0.29	*−5.52*
IHORIZON	0.22	*2.22*	0.21	*2.57*	0.15	*2.02*	0.15	*3.91*
STAGE2	−0.25	*−1.01*	−0.18	*−0.87*				
BENCHMARK2	0.32	*0.95*						
FXPOLICY2	−1.39	*−4.25*	−1.33	*−5.52*	−1.29	*−5.59*	−1.29	*−10.8*
AREAS2	−1.46	*−2.88*	−1.37	*−3.84*	−1.26	*−3.40*	−1.26	*−6.58*
AREAS3	0.30	*0.61*						
AUTDECISION2	1.09	*2.89*	0.78	*2.54*	1.11	*4.85*	1.11	*9.37*
AUTIMPLEMENT2	0.81	*1.69*	0.54	*1.75*				
AUTIMPLEMENT3	0.32	*1.20*						
ERRISK	0.15	*0.57*						
HTUSE	−0.11	*−1.24*						
R^2	0.88		0.80		0.73		0.73	

financial tools is difficult in the region under study.[7] As a consequence, these variables were dropped from future regressions.

A second regression was run (Reg 2) including the remaining nine variables. The results in this case show that *ORIGIN*, *OWNERSHIP*, *IHORIZON*, *FXPOLICY2* and *AREAS2* are statistically significant and that there is also some role for *AUTDECISION2*. With these results, a third regression (Reg 3) was run including these six variables. This model presents clear statistically significant coefficients for the six independent variables and therefore became the 'preferred' version (the model is also significant at the 0.005 level and explains almost 60 per cent of the variation in the exchange rate exposure). The analysis of the results can be seen below:

- *ORIGIN* has a relatively small positive relation with the foreign exchange exposure, an outcome contrary to what was expected. This variable was included following what was suggested by Hakkarainen et al. (1998), and a negative or even neutral relation was expected as the countries of origin have a relatively high tradition of international operations. Even considering that the EU is the largest investor in the Mercosur + Chile region, this outcome could reflect the relatively short experience acquired in the region (except for some British companies and a few other exceptions), and the fact that these investments are dominated by Spanish companies (where companies started their internationalization to Latin America only around ten years ago). This relatively short amount of experience could have resulted in an unexpected environment where the traditional tools used in other countries/regions might be less effective in the region under study. In addition, it provides evidence that more research on FX exposure in international contexts and also studying MNEs from outside the US can give better insights into the relation between unexpected changes in the value of currencies and market returns.
- *OWNERSHIP* shows the expected negative relation with the exposure to variations in the exchange rate. This could be interpreted, following what is suggested in the literature, as the transfer of the parent's advantages strengthens the subsidiaries' position in dealing with changes in the value of different currencies.
- *IHORIZON* (meaning of long-term investments for the company) presents a positive relation, contrary to what was expected.

This estimate suggests that those companies that declared intentions to stay longer seem to have higher exposure to changes in the exchange rate value. This could be interpreted as meaning that companies with shorter horizons may design and operate structures that are more flexible and therefore easier to adapt to changes in the environment, or even leave the country if the situation becomes difficult. This is relevant in the context of the emerging markets under study as some companies drastically reduced/adapted their operations in the region during the troubled period (1998/99 to 2004/05),[8] a decision that could have helped them to reduce the impact of the crises on their cash flows.

- *FXPOLICY2* (development of an exchange rate hedging policy) has the expected negative relation in comparison with *FXPOLICY1*, the reference group (no formal policy). This coefficient indicates that companies with formal exchange rate policies have a lower exposure to foreign exchange risk than companies without such a policy (controlling for other independent variables in the equation).
- *AREAS2* (foreign exchange exposure assessed by areas related to finance) presents a negative relation in comparison with the reference group *AREAS1* (foreign exchange exposure assessed by other areas in the company), meaning that companies where the assessment is carried out by finance + other related areas (risk management, treasury, projects, accounting, planning, etc) have a foreign exchange exposure 1.14 lower than companies where this assessment is also the responsibility of other areas in the company, holding constant the other independent variables. This outcome is contrary to what the literature suggests and is also an unexpected one as a proposition of this work was that other areas of the company (mainly operations and marketing) should participate in the assessment of foreign exchange rate risk. However, the fact that *AREAS3* (assessment only by finance) and *HTUSE* (relative use of hedging tools) do not have an impact on the foreign exchange exposure in the sample seem to corroborate that foreign exchange exposure assessed only by finance and using mostly financial tools appears to be less effective in the region under study and, as a consequence, other strategies/techniques need to be used in this context.
- *AUTDECISION2* (medium decentralization of decision-making for hedging), in comparison with *AUTDECISION1* (high decentralization, the reference group) has the predicted positive relationship.

This means that companies with middle decentralization show a 0.94 higher exposure to foreign exchange movements than companies with high decentralization (controlling for independent variables in the equation). In the context of this work and considering the previous findings (mainly *IHORIZON*), this result can be interpreted as showing that subsidiaries with more autonomy to make decisions on hedging initiatives seem to deal better with the effects of (unexpected and/or high) variations in the exchange rate.

6.2.1 Robustness checks

Panels B and C in Table 6.2 record the results of the same regressions described above (Reg 1 to Reg 3), but they change the choice of dependent variable to the absolute value of the t-statistic, $|t|$, and to the absolute value of the foreign exchange exposure coefficient, $|\beta_{fx}|$, respectively. As explained above, the cross-sectional regression was planned to be run again in order to check for the robustness of the findings to other definitions of foreign exchange exposure. As can be seen, the results are similar to those presented in Panel A, providing support to the analysis and findings described before. Reg 4 in Panels A, B, and C presents the results of a regression of the 'preferred' model but using a sample artificially increased[9] to test the significance of the findings obtained from the smaller sample used in previous regressions. The analysis of the regression equations upon which this analysis is based indicates that 'increasing the size of the sample in this way will not affect the size or direction of the correlations between the variables because the pattern of the data has not changed, but it will make the correlations significant' (Cramer, 2004). The results obtained in Reg 4 using the three different independent variables (Panels A, B, and C) are similar to the ones obtained in Reg 3 (simultaneous and stepwise), giving support to the statistical significance of the findings of the previous analysis.[10]

The model was also checked for the regression assumptions. The first check was specification, the omission or inclusion of irrelevant variables and the selection of an incorrect functional form. This check can be seen in the process from Reg 1 to Reg 3 (simultaneous and stepwise regressions) from where the preferred model emerged. This process was carried out to test the robustness of the model, to avoid losses in the accuracy of the relevant coefficients' estimates, and to avoid a biased coefficient by estimating a linear function when the relationship between variables was nonlinear (Schroeder et al., 1986). Secondly, different measures were put in place to avoid measurement errors, such as back translations and the pilot testing of the questionnaire, interviews carried out by the same person in similar contexts, and the use of reliable sources to obtain data. Third, autocorrelation was checked by calculating the Durbin–Watson coefficient.[11] Fourthly, t-statistics were adjusted by a heteroskedasticity correction in the regressions (White, 1980)[12] to test if error terms depend upon factors included in the analysis. Finally, multicollinearity was tested through an analysis of the correlation coefficients between the variables in the model where only *AUTDECISION2* showed a relatively high statistical significant correlation with *ORIGIN* and *FXPOLICY2*, but they were included as they are dummy variables measuring different data. Eigenvalues were also tested and provided similar conclusions.

6.3 Qualitative analysis: results

The qualitative analysis was based on the data collected in interviews carried out between February and August 2005 in different countries with senior managers from European companies with subsidiaries in Mercosur countries and Chile. It is important to highlight that the researcher took the position of an external and objective observer of facts, events, decisions, strategies, lessons, and so on, experienced by companies during the period and in the region under analysis, as well as how they were affected by changes in the environment (especially the variations in the exchange rate). The period under study went from the mid-1990s to 2005; some participants were able to talk about the first years of the 1990s, and some were not in the post during some of the years under study, in the latter cases, the focus was on the actions taken by the company before her/his arrival.

It is also important to mention that the interviews in Argentina were, unintentionally, centred around the political and economic crisis that affected the country from the end of 2001 as it seems that the consequences and memories of this crisis were still fresh in the minds of the participants; this was judged as positive because it gave the opportunity to understand what happened in a very extreme situation. The interviews in Argentina were analysed taking into consideration this situation to keep the comparison neutral.

Table 6.3 Cross-sectional stepwise regression

	Dependent variable β_{fx}											
	Reg 1				Reg 3				Reg 4			
	Order	R^2	F	p	Order	R^2	F	p	Order	R^2	F	p
INDUSTRY												
CURRENCIES												
ORIGIN	1	0.15	4.39	0.05	1	0.15	4.39	0.05	1	0.13	11.45	0.00
COUNTRIES												
OWNERSHIP									5	0.67	16.43	0.00
IHORIZON									6	0.73	15.29	0.00
STAGE2												
BENCHMARK2												
FXPOLICY2	2	0.30	4.72	0.04	2	0.30	4.72	0.04	2	0.30	17.47	0.00
AREAS2									4	0.60	15.19	0.00
AREAS3												
AUTDECISION2									3	0.52	33.98	0.00
AUTIMPLEMENT2	3	0.41	4.34	0.05								
AUTIMPLEMENT3												
ERRISK												
HTUSE												

The analysis of the data showed the following initial categories: risk coverage, volatility, institutions, local knowledge, managing organizations in emerging markets, and consequences of the devaluations.

6.3.1 Category 1: exchange rate risk coverage

In all of the reviews the first comment received with regard to risk coverage was that the Latin American economy (LA) works in US dollars; in fact, one participant even observed that 'customers are scared of contracts in euros'. Although it is generally accepted that LA's economies have been linked to that of the US, it was an unexpected outcome to see that most of the European companies in the sample use the US dollar for reference in their operations. For example, one company with no important presence in the US market observed that they 'have balanced their foreign exchange (FX) risk with their investments in US dollars from LA, their investments in euros in Europe, and their investments in pound sterling in the UK'.[13] In this context, many companies value their internal transfer prices in US dollars, where the parent absorbs the difference between the American currency and the euro, and the subsidiary the variations between the dollar and the local currency.

Companies selling highly differentiated products were able to set their prices in US dollars; but this strategy was effective only on those products where the differentiation is based upon specific technologies (and therefore when the competition is minimal or even non-existent). Companies offering products and services where the differentiation is based on other factors stated that they were unable to pass through the variations in the value of the local currency. This is in line with what is suggested in the literature (see section 3.3.2). This strategy of setting prices in US dollars was also used in marketing-driven companies (with products differentiated by well-known brands) that prioritize their high-end positioning with a policy of not adjusting their international prices. This is also in line with the hedging strategies suggested in the literature (see section 3.3.4); however, in these cases, the companies recognised that this strategy has not been effective as the demand for their products plummeted (up to 85 per cent) as a consequence of devaluations in the local currency (coincidentally, the companies that reported having followed this strategy also showed, in general, the highest exposure to foreign exchange risk, β_{fx}, see Table 6.1).

Companies with differentiated local products (around 15 per cent of the sample), like wines, started a process of internationalization after the devaluation altered their cost structures; their aim now is to get a balance between exports and imports to compensate the materials bought abroad and expressed in foreign currency. This is a kind of operational hedging, which is recognised in the literature and was explained in a previous chapter (see section 3.3.3); however, although these companies are part of larger parent companies with operations in many countries, it is interesting to see that this was a reactive decision. It was made after the devaluation of the local currency and, as a result, after having assumed most of the associated costs. In addition, this decision implied, in most of the cases, a change in the business model, as these companies with established distribution networks and relevant market shares in domestic markets needed to learn to commercialize their products in new and more competitive international markets.

Participants recognised that financial tools to hedge FX risk are not used widely in LA companies. Some parent companies hedge their flows centrally (reflected in variable *HTUSE* of the quantitative analysis) as they have a central treasury to deal with this and other risks. However, subsidiaries operating in LA seem to find it difficult to hedge their FX with financial tools as most of the time they are not available in many local currencies ('it is almost impossible to find a counterpart in need of local currency'[14]) or because 'the cost of the financial tools is more expensive than the expected variations in the exchange rate'.[15] Another hedging strategy that is difficult to find in LA companies is that of funding in local currency, this is 'because local banks do not have the capacity to finance large investment projects in the local currency'[16] or 'because the periods offered to repay the loans do not give the project time to develop'.[17] For this reason, the participants said, many parent companies assume the debt in their local currencies and transfer these funds to the subsidiary; but they also recognised that the FX risk is not hedged in those projects with expected incomes in local currencies. This is an important difference to what is suggested in the literature where most of the hedging is based on financial instruments (see section 3.3.1); on the contrary, it gives support to the main argument of this work that a broader approach is needed to protect the value of the foreign investments in emerging markets.

6.3.2 Category 2: volatility

The overwhelming majority (more than 90 per cent) of the participants said that volatility in the value of the exchange rate impacts and has impacted both their growth and profitability. These comments contrast with the answers received in one of the structured questions, where 100 per cent of the respondents said that currency is not an issue and the most important issue when deciding investments abroad are the business prospects. In this sense, a highly repeated comment in the interviews was that the 'original projections for the company were too high', expecting, for example, 'annual returns of 20 per cent sustained during the first five years of operations'.[18] Two companies that entered at the beginning of the 1990s recognised that 'they achieved this return in the first two years',[19] but then the situation changed and the returns were revised downwards; the companies that made important investments (around 40 per cent of the sample) after 1995/1996 said that they had never achieved the original projections. In all of the cases, once they started their operations they adjusted their expectations down in line with this reality.

The question after this comment was: what is the overall result of the company's experience in the countries under study? The answer in more than 90 per cent of the cases was that they were not sure if they have earned any money, Brazil only few gains, Argentina mainly losses, and Chile gains ('but Chile is too small to make a difference'); Mexico (although not one of the countries studied) was mentioned as the place where they had earned the most (but after that, some participants said 'we are now waiting for a new Tequila' in reference to the Mexican crisis of 1994). This response was particularly surprising in the stratum of Spanish companies (with high exposures in Argentina; see Arahuetes & Casilda, 2004), only one said that they sold off their Argentine subsidiary in 1998 (before the problems in Brazil and Argentina) 'at a loss'[20] because they foresaw difficult times ahead and used this experience to set up subsidiaries in other LA countries; as a result of this strategy, this company can show, in general, a successful story.

Volatility also seems to affect companies in other ways. One of the participants said that 'volatility is a disincentive that offsets all the incentives offered by a country'[21] which makes companies (especially local managers) adopt a shorter-term perspective. In fact, some interviewees mentioned the longer-term view given by their European parent as an important contribution to the subsidiary. Another problem seems to be the difficulty to make plans, budgets, and control standards to assess performance; for example, one respondent said that 'my company makes annual budgets with the expected exchange rate from the top ten US banks operating in the region, and the experience shows that none of these projections were accurate in the last seven years when we started with this process'.[22]

A third problem is that it gives companies a false sense of competitiveness as, when the Argentine and Brazilian currencies were overvalued as the result of being pegged to the US dollar in the 1990s, companies struggled to survive and keep their products in the market (even domestic markets). On the contrary, following the big devaluations of 1999 and 2001, companies found it very easy to sell their products abroad. 'But now, as the devaluation advantage is over, we do not know if we are in the right position to compete; it is like taking drugs, they give a sense of relief at the beginning but then you do not know where you wake up. The worst thing is that this is addictive for some companies.'[23]

Fourthly, volatility in the exchange rate also generates variations in the quality of products. In an increasingly integrated world, products are made of materials from different parts of the world. When the value of the currency changes, the cost structure of many products also changes, prompting companies to find local (international) suppliers, especially for those products where it is not possible to pass through the higher prices or where competition forces the prices down. Many of the participants working in manufacturing companies (around 30 per cent of the sample) said that a possible way to overcome this problem is by integrating the value chain, but they also recognised that the company, as a whole, still loses (wins) as the final price is lower (higher) due to the devaluation (revaluation) of the local currency in relation to that of the origin of the materials.

6.3.3 Category 3: institutions

This category includes the quality, stability, and strength to enforce the law of institutions in those countries included in the study. The main targets of the comments were the regulatory agencies, but other government bodies were also included. In the case of Argentina, most of the government (at the national and provincial levels) was targeted, mainly due to the many changes in decisions and policies; after all, this country changed five presidents in one week at the end of 2001!

The great majority of the participants agreed that the quality of the institutions is key to the success or failure of their businesses in LA. In this sense, they recognised that institutions impact and have impacted the profitability of their companies; within this framework, they also agreed that this impact has been, in general, a negative one. The main reason they used to explain this situation was that, in LA, institutions generally are not independent from political power and, as a consequence, the political environment sets the business conditions. This was very clearly illustrated by a participant, born in Mexico, with many years of experience as a director for the Latin American region of a UK company: 'we all know that the application of the law in LA has different shades'. Another good example came from a French company that gives autonomy to its subsidiaries in each LA country to set their own strategic plans, the only condition was that each planning cycle should start at the beginning of every presidential term and should be done for the same number of years that the presidents remain in office (for example, in Argentina for four years, or Chile for six years, now changed), in order to ensure that no changes in the political environment will affect their business plans.

Many participants also stated that institutions affect the profitability of their companies by failing to control the shadow economy. For example, interviewees estimated that those companies that avoid taxes and contributions to social security have a cost advantage of between 25 and 30 per cent. A third area of impact from institutions came from the changes in government officials resulting from the weak independence in political power referred to earlier. The problem is that every new person taking over a position in a government agency is likely to change everything (according to the new and changing political environment), continually making every negotiation and every relationship begin again. Many situations were cited in order to illustrate this problem – an extreme example was given by a Finnish company based in Chile developing a project in Ecuador. After two years negotiating a project with a government official, the deal was agreed and the president of the country wanted to sign the contract in a public act for which the Chairman and CEO of company were invited to Ecuador. The company's officers left Europe on a Friday; when they arrived in Ecuador on Saturday, the president had resigned and there was no contract to sign. After that, the company tried to keep the project alive in the hope that the new government policies would be similar; however, after two additional years of negotiations they decided to quit.

The institutions also played an important role in the form of regulatory agencies for those companies operating in regulated industries. In this case, participants also recognised that the quality of the regulator defines the success of their operations. In this context, the comments seem to indicate that a strong and close relation with the regulator is critical for the business and that they have learnt that local managers develop better relations with regulators because it is easy for them to understand the 'current and past environment where the regulators make decisions'.[24] In fact, the relationship with the regulators is the responsibility of a local manager in all the cases in the sample except one. This one company claims that it has successfully applied a 'model developed in the parent to deal at the subsidiary level with local regulators and is based on very strict self-regulations, even tougher than what is requested in many countries'.[25] This last example shows that it seems that there are two possible strategies to deal with local regulators: on the one hand, a local manager understanding the local environment; on the other hand, a model developed in Europe based on very strict self-regulations. A third strategy was applied by one of the companies in the past, they decided to 'increase our share in the industry over 50% to gain relative weight to deal with the regulator; we increased the participation in our company and bought others to reach this level, as well as we sold off those businesses where getting this level was not possible'.[26]

In particular, companies in Argentina also reported different situations where institutions affected the profitability of the European companies in the study. This can be seen in the privatized public utility companies as 'the new (from 2003) government seems to prefer local owners rather than the international companies operating these companies since the 1990s',[27] as was expressed by one of the interviewees. This apparent preference has ended up with many investors selling off their subsidiaries in the country and setting claims in the World Bank's International Centre for Settlement of Investment Disputes (ICSID) against Argentina. This was the case of EDF selling

Edenor and Edemsa, France Telecom selling Telecom Argentina, or Suez leaving Aguas Argentinas, among others. There are more than 30 demands accepted by the ICSID valued at around US$20 billion and around another 70 waiting to be analysed for around US$80 billion, making Argentina the country with the highest number of claims in the world. In this context, it is important to mention that the large Spanish investors have agreed with the Argentine government to continue operating (and keeping ownership of) the privatized companies followed by a promise to withdraw their claims from the ICSID.

Most of these disputes have their origins in the privatization agreements signed in the 1990s (when the Argentine peso was pegged to the US dollar) that included an indexation clause linked to the price of the dollar. In 2001, the law that finished the peg also said that all contracts (not only those with the utility companies) indexed by US dollars (or any other foreign currency) became unlawful. As a consequence of the change in the value of the currency, the companies asked the government to increase the price of the services according to the US dollar as was originally agreed, accusing the government of changing the rules. On the other hand, the government said that the law should be applied equally to all the citizens and, as a result, there will not be any exceptions. It is not the intention here to discuss and analyse the particularities of this dispute as it is out of the scope of the present study and because there are many specialized publications on the matter. The main objective of its inclusion is to introduce very interesting and heated discussions with the interviewees.

On the one hand, around half of the participants with operations in Argentina (mostly European managers working either at the parent or in the Latin American country) defined the government's position as 'outrageous' because it did not respect the law or any previous agreement. They blamed this decision on the poor performance of their companies which, three years after the devaluation (the Argentine peso went from Ar$1/US$1 to Ar$3/US$1 in 15 days and has kept this value until the time of the interviews), still have the same prices, but with many costs indexed in foreign currency and an aggregate inflation of over 50 per cent. They also claimed that the government is 'asking for the investments in US$ committed in the contract, but we do not have the resources and our parent does not want to give us the money until this situation becomes clearer; for example, the government wants these investments but it does not pay us the subsidies agreed in the contract!'[28]

On the other hand, the remaining 50 per cent of the participants (mainly Argentine senior managers working for the European companies, many of them having started in their positions after the devaluation) said that 'relying only on the contract was naïve! Not because it is not possible to trust in the government, but because nobody can imagine in any country that the government will accept an increase of 300 per cent in the public services in the middle of one of the worst economic crises in modern economic history'.[29] The main problem, another participant continued, 'was that none of these companies were prepared for a crisis that had been waiting to explode since 1999 [the devaluation in Brazil after many years pegged to the US dollar]; I didn't see any proposal to the government on how to deal with the problem, now it is easier to blame the government'.[30]

In the context of this work, the important part of this situation is that all of these companies, without exception, did not cover their FX risk because they relied entirely on the indexation clause in the contract. This situation shows, once again, that hedging against FX risk is more complex in emerging markets because the same tools are not widely available (as discussed previously in section 6.3.1) and that aspects that could be taken for granted in developed economies would need to be assessed in detail in less developed countries before any decision could be made. In addition, this also proved that hedging using financial tools could not have prevented these companies from assuming the losses due to the changes in the value of the foreign currency.

Participants working in the remaining companies (not privatized public utilities) also mentioned other problems that were related to the variations in the exchange rate caused by institutions in Argentina that affected their cash flows in local and foreign currencies. One example of this was that after the devaluation, the Argentine government set an export levy on all the products sold abroad 'when exports was the only way for us to survive as the domestic demand plunged'.[31] Other similar decisions by the government that affected the profitability of companies were the restrictions on the export of petroleum and the freezing of the domestic price of fuel; 'just when the international price is reaching US$60, we are only receiving US$24!'[32] The government also set a levy on alcohol,

> we had the problem of a very depressed domestic market and out of the blue the government set this levy; fortunately, after a year of negotiations, our industry agreed with the government to withdraw the levy and in exchange we committed a certain amount of investments. This was a success as we needed the investments anyway. The problem was with our parent in France, the budget for the year included the levy, but then when we presented the annual figures the levy was replaced by investments and an explanation of the negotiation; they could not believe that we negotiated taxes versus investments![33]

6.3.4 Category 4: local knowledge

Over 90 per cent of the participants stated explicitly or implicitly that local knowledge was key in order to: (i) understand and anticipate the crises and their effects; (ii) adapt products and management practices ('because Europeans do not always understand LA's culture'[34]); (iii) strengthen relations with the regulator; (iv) understand the local market; and (v) grow in an uncertain environment. In many cases, this local knowledge took the form of a local partner with an important – but not controlling – participation in the capital of the company. The local partners seemed to have been successful in giving the companies in the sample a Latin American perspective; as an interviewee put it, 'the local partner offered a fusion with the local reality, it first amended the projections made by the parent and second included the crises in the business plans. The parent made wrong assessments of emerging markets'.[35]

The local partners were mentioned as being crucial in privatized companies during the process of negotiating prices of public services in Argentina (explained in the previous section) as 'they speak the same language of the government'.[36] This is consistent with the answers received to the question in the structured section on ownership policy. In fact, the director of a French company, looking retrospectively, recognised that 'it was a mistake having 90 per cent of the company, with a local investor the situation would have been different; it is a mistake in LA to have majority control'. These comments are in line with what the literature says under the resource-based view of the firm in emerging markets research stream (described in section 2.8).

A final comment, also in the context of the Argentinean crisis, was that

> European managers working in this country did not show the same commitment to face the problems, as soon as they saw the social mess, the riots, the five presidents, the kidnaps, the insecurity, etc.; they wanted to leave the country. A new problem arose last year, they came back, which signalled a glass ceiling for the good local people that helped this company to survive during the worst years of the crises. Now, these persons are leaving us, they are going with the competitors.[37]

6.3.5 Category 5: managing organizations in emerging markets

This category tries to incorporate the comments received from the participants about the particular challenges they are facing for operating in an emerging context. A recurrent comment was that 'the price [level] does not give space for big investments; first it is difficult to achieve our sales target, and second it is difficult to get a big margin in a low income market'.[38] This idea was also present in the privatized public utilities, they said that 'the privatisation models applied in LA were those exported from the UK, and you know what has happened there'[39] referring to the low levels of investments in public services in Great Britain in recent years.

Another challenge identified by these companies was the risk of economic integration: 'when you integrate two emerging markets you are doubling the risk; when there is a crisis in Brazil, it automatically becomes a crisis in Argentina, and vice versa'.[40] To this comment, a participant added, 'Mercosur does not exist, Argentina did not do anything after the Brazil devaluation and we were flooded by Brazilian products, but in 2002 [after the devaluation in Argentina] Brazil set restrictions to our products, just when we needed them the most. Now, Argentina is setting restrictions to many Brazilian products!'[41] An integrated manufacturing company with operations in both countries explained that 'we needed to be very creative [in exporting and importing materials and final products between the two countries] to avoid disrupting our production process; today the process is completely different than what was originally planned'.[42] It seems that, in addition to the consequences of the crises, the devaluation tempted governments to set restrictions to their trade partners to protect the local producers, but these measures also affected those local producers that based their productive process on the advantages offered by each country.

Companies that were trying to sell their products abroad also found that 'the products from emerging markets have a perception of low quality and low standardisation'[43] in developed countries. This perception seemed to become more difficult to overcome in the years after the devaluations. For example, a company explained that 'this was a problem when we decided to sell abroad; we found that many people from Brazil and Argentina, taking advantage of the devaluated prices, were selling products without a clear definition of quality and service'.[44] Two of the wineries in the sample said that they were able to overcome this problem as they use their parents' international distribution channels, but the other companies recognised that 'it takes a lot of time and hard work to develop credibility and confidence with a customer abroad'.[45]

This perception of low confidence was also present in the relationship with foreign suppliers; as a participant put it, 'we do not have a problem because they know that we are part of the [X] group, but we know that our suppliers and contractors suffer this problem; on top of that, our market is so small for them that the risks associated with the operation sometimes are higher than the benefits'.[46] In this sense, most of the managers in Argentina said that it was very difficult for them to import materials after the start of the crisis because the way the country managed the default of its sovereign debt appeared in all the newspapers in the world. One participant illustrated this situation very clearly,

> on 31/12/01 at 6p.m. a big supplier from the US called to my mobile, he said I have just seen one of your last five presidents on TV, he said that your country will not pay to foreign creditors while laughing; are you going to pay us? I immediately said yes, why not, we have been doing business for a long time... But the problem was that, after this conversation, the government abandoned the peg

> to the dollar so we had to negotiate the payment in local currency. He always reminded me that I had given him my word...[47]

Another company in Argentina said that they had to call a foreign supplier explaining that a subsidiary of a [well-known] European group is the final customer of a purchase order received from Y [one of the company's suppliers].

Some participants attributed this low level of standardization to the fact that people in these emerging countries are not exposed to the relatively higher and demanding standards of many developed economies.

> How can you expect that someone will perform at her highest in her work if what she sees everyday is below average standards? Take a walk near to this office, the cleanliness on the streets, the quality of the service in the shop across this street, the public transport, etc., almost everything operates at different standards than those in Europe.[48]

This is a very interesting and revealing comment because it is an issue that is rarely mentioned in the literature. Another reason mentioned as a possible source of the low standardization of the quality is that of low levels of qualifications. Companies recognised that 'for top positions there are good professionals, many of them with studies abroad, but for middle and operative jobs we always have problems'.[49] In this sense, one major problem is that the majority of the workforce do not speak English, making internal communication and training more difficult as many of the companies in the sample use English as their main language (even companies from continental Europe; the exception was the Spanish enterprises).

Another challenge faced by some of the subsidiaries in LA is that of explaining the local environment to their parent companies in Europe. Many comments in this area were discussed during the interviews: 'it is very difficult for us to explain to them the problems we have; for example, how can you explain the power, and sometimes extortions, of the unions?';[50] 'there was a picket in front of our factory, the problem was that the police were giving support to them!';[51] 'our parent company does not understand our inflation levels, they did not approve a 12 per cent rise in salaries for the next year when inflation was 12 per cent';[52] 'during the crisis [in Argentina] our [French] parent company forced us to work only with French banks, but these banks were not prepared to accept Patacones [one of more than 20 quasi-currencies issued by local governments during the crisis to cancel debts] so we spent more than a month without paying in part of our sales!'[53]

6.3.6 Category 6: consequences of the devaluations

The first and most important consequences mentioned by the participants were changes in the composition of demand and in the habits of consumers. In this sense, a wine company illustrated the situation by saying that its 'traditional market disappeared from one day to the other! Suddenly there was no more middle class';[54] one of its competitors explained that 'now [four years after the devaluation in Argentina] you can see a rise in the demand of our top wines, but the consumption is different, it is not about status and social occasions any more, the consumption is private, with a feeling that they can have it again; but, as you can imagine, we are still not selling as many bottles as five years ago'.[55] This change in the composition of demand can also be seen in a comment from an insurance company,

> we first replaced all the annual policies for quarterly ones, and then we stopped issuing policies on certain models of cars as they became targets of spare parts mafias, their brands abandoned the country and the only way to find spare parts was by importing them, which was very expensive, or by buying them in the black market which came from stolen cars. The number of stolen cars was unbelievably high![56]

The consequence of this change in demand made some companies seek out new markets abroad using their parent's distribution channels ('by doing so, we lost independence as now we depend on the sales coming from the parent'[57]), or try to find new segments in the market ('our hotel chain is specialised in business travellers, but after the devaluation in Argentina there were no more business travellers, so we attracted the tourists that flooded the country, it was odd to see children playing in the business centre!'[58]). In many cases, these changes in demand and target market, along with the changes in the supply chain (described in section 6.3.1), forced companies to change their business model. In other words, as a consequence of the variations in the price of the foreign currency, the business model of many of these subsidiaries operating in LA (and imported from the parent in Europe) was changed due to the new conditions in the environment. For example, a subsidiary of a technology company started local technology developments to satisfy the demand from its customers due to the high costs of developing solutions in Europe (as was always the case) and the low level of price competition from local suppliers. This situation shows that financial tools are not effective to hedge variations in the exchange rate in LA and that an approach considering all the areas in a company could be more effective.

This adaptation of the business model was possible as most of the parent companies gave total autonomy to their subsidiaries 'to do what they need to do in order to protect the company'.[59] This autonomy reached extremes in some cases where, for example, the subsidiaries were written off from the parent's balance sheet or when the parent did not agree to give any kind of financial support (in one of the latter cases, the person responsible for the LA region had to tell the subsidiary's employees 'there will not be lay-offs, but I cannot guarantee the salaries'[60]). As a counterpart of this autonomy, many companies ought 'to rationalise the operations as the only way to survive without external support';[61] the unexpected outcome of this effort was that, in most cases, by the time of the interviews the participants were proud to say that their subsidiaries were among the most efficient within their groups, and that few companies were exporting the new practices and local developments to their parents. An interesting third consequence was that three of the managers during the crises were promoted to the parent in Europe, one of them to deal with a crisis in Russia.

In spite of this relatively good news, due to the write-offs and/or the devalued price of the subsidiaries, the Latin American region lost weight in the balance sheets and, also, in the decisions of the parent companies. In the majority of the cases, the participants said that now LA is not the star emerging market any more, the region has been replaced by Eastern Europe and Asia. This is reflected in the assignation of resources, the priority to launch new products, the expansion plans, or the efforts to make local developments. One of the participants illustrated this situation by saying that 'some years ago our company [which operates in Brazil and Argentina] was requested the same return as the top priority markets, 6.2 per cent; now our parent asks us the highest possible return in the whole group: 19.5 per cent. You can imagine that only a few projects can be developed with this number'.[62] Many participants also said that the priority in LA now switched to Mexico and to only very good opportunities in Brazil, and most of the Spanish companies said that 'future investments will go to investment grade countries'.[63]

6.3.7 Relations and interrelations among the six categories

The analysis of the six categories described in the previous sections gives the opportunity to find relations and interrelations among them. The first interrelation is among the local partners (local knowledge), the high expectations from the parent companies (volatility) and the difficulty of setting out plans and budgets (volatility). The comments from the participants tend to indicate that local knowledge (in the form of local partners or local managers) can make more accurate projections in LA economies. The claim that only local managers can make more precise projections, although a commonsensical statement in the sense that the closer the knowledge of a situation, the better its descriptions, is very strong and difficult to accept in the absence of sufficient supporting evidence. For this reason, it will be used only in very specific contexts in future analyses.

The second relation found is between low levels of standardization in the quality of products (volatility) and the changes in the business models (consequences of the devaluations). A third relation was also found between the levy on exports (institutions) and the changes in the business model (consequences of the devaluations). These relations should be of concern to companies, both those already operating, and also those planning investments in emerging markets. They need to find suitable ways to protect their competitive advantage, their main source of profits, against variations in the value of the currency.

A fourth relation encountered is between the close relation with the regulator (local knowledge) and the quality of the regulator (institutions). It is possible to see the sense of this relation; however, two other successful strategies to deal with regulators were presented. In this sense, companies operating in emerging markets need to set a strategy to deal with local regulators that balances the needs of the host society (represented by the regulator) with the plans of the company. Although a local manager is the most widely used strategy in the companies in the sample, it is not clear that this is the best strategy to get this balance.

6.3.8 Concepts arising from the analysis of qualitative data

This section will present the final steps of the qualitative data analysis described in section A1.7.2. It will attempt to conceptualize the data collected from the interviews and coded and categorized above. In the context of this work, the effects of exchange rate variations on companies' performance, the concepts identified throughout the analysis are:

a. *Familiarity:* become acquainted with the country in which the subsidiary will operate, an idea that builds upon that of local knowledge mentioned by the participants. It includes an in-depth knowledge and understanding of the local history and culture in order to avoid surprises by sudden changes in the business environment and to develop strong relations with the regulators. It also includes the planning of different social and institutional scenarios, along with possible response strategies. In this sense, participants highlighted the need to be aware that the systems behind the institutions, business networks, and tools to diminish transaction costs, function differently in emerging economies than could generally be expected in developed countries. This *Familiarity* can take the form of local partners, local managers, or a reasonable period of time studying the country before setting a whole subsidiary, along with a constant exchange of persons (and information) between the parent and the subsidiary once it is operating.
b. *Inclusiveness:* running a business in an emerging market seems to be different from that in developed economies, according to the participants. The (relative weakness of) institutions seem to have important impacts on the organization's performance, the transaction costs tend to be higher, and the competitive advantages appear to give only a relative superiority. Participants also said that the sources of impact on the performance of their companies usually came from the changes in the business environment. This situation calls for proactive/flexible managers, considering all the

factors (internal and external) that could affect the company's operation, and designing inclusive strategies among the different areas in the organization; especially as it seems that the tools generally used to deal with similar situations in developed countries are less effective in these developing markets. Participants also highlighted the need to avoid the short-term perspective trap, which can occur while muddling through after changes in the environment, and shifts from the original strategic plan.

c. *Prudence:* participants stated that the costs (and risks) of doing business in emerging markets can offset the expected high returns. The projected sales are usually difficult to achieve and hidden [transaction] costs can make it more difficult to obtain high margins. In addition, the volatility (political, economic, and social) of these markets appears as a potential risk to ruin even the best business plan. In other words, the expected high returns associated with emerging markets can be achieved during good years, but sudden changes in the market can turn this situation overnight, making the average/long-term performance of the subsidiary suffer. One way to face this is by testing cash flows to the limit, constructing different scenarios and assessing them in a conservative way, measuring carefully every potential risk and penalizing the (relatively high) projected sales.
d. *Liability of origin*: participants said that selling products from emerging markets abroad (especially in developed countries) seems to be more difficult than what would generally be expected. They suggested that this is principally because emerging countries' products appear to have a perception of low-quality standardization, a situation that can worsen during currency crises as many companies and individuals follow opportunistic behaviours and use the devaluation advantage to sell any kind of relatively low-price product without much concern for quality standards and/or long-term relations. This makes it hard and costly to start an export operation after a devaluation of the host country's currency. This concept also includes the low qualifications of the labour force in certain areas, and the difficulty of hedging FX using financial instruments as they are not widely available. This liability should be included in the business plans if the subsidiary intends to sell abroad, especially on the marketing and finance sides. It will also need to be reflected in the training programmes for

local employees and the knowledge transfer strategy of the parent company.

e. *Open eyes:* emerging markets can continue to offer good business opportunities, even during and after currency crises. Changes in the composition of the demand and in the consumers' habits, one of the consequences of the crises, usually imply new segments and niches waiting to be exploited. In this sense, subsidiaries can use their assets and knowledge to develop new products and services tailored to these new potential clients provided that they have enough autonomy from the parent to do so and that the business models are not affected. These local developments can also be seen as a way to acquire a better understanding and adaptation to the host country.

6.4 Mixed methods: results

Figure 6.1 shows a summary of the findings obtained in the quantitative and qualitative analyses presented in sections 6.2 and 6.3.

Figure 6.1 gives a summary of the findings obtained in the previous analyses; it illustrates that five variables from the quantitative analysis and five concepts from the qualitative analysis have an impact on companies' performance (in the form of market value). In addition, these findings tend to cross-validate and corroborate each other; in fact, some of them also tend to be complementary, like *AUTDECISION1* and *Open Eyes*, *Familiarity* and *OWNERSHIP*, and *IHORIZON* and *Inclusiveness*.

This empirical evidence shows that ten variables/concepts, which encompass different functional areas, have an influence on firms' FX; therefore, managers may minimize the effects of unanticipated changes in the value of EM's currencies by including these functional areas in the decision-making of hedging strategies. These results, presented in Figure 6.1, provide support to the main argument of this work, that a holistic approach to hedging (including the different functional areas, mainly finance, marketing, operations management, and marketing) against unexpected variations in the exchange rate is expected to contribute to reducing the impact that these variations have on the value of companies with foreign investments in emerging markets.

Quantitative analysis findings	Qualitative analysis findings
OWNERSHIP: the transfer of the parent's advantages strengthens the subsidiaries' position to deal with changes in the value of different currencies.	*Familiarity*: with the host country's history and culture, local knowledge to understand the business environment and develop relations with regulators, plan different social and business scenarios. Local partners or local managers.
IHORIZON (meaning of long-term investments for the company): companies in the sample with shorter horizons may design and operate structures that are more flexible and easier to adapt to changes in the environment.	*Inclusiveness*: weaknesses of institutions have impacts on performance, transaction costs tend to be higher, and the competitive advantages appear to give only a relative superiority. Avoid the short-term perspective trap.
FXPOLICY2 (development of an exchange rate hedging policy): companies in the sample with formal policies seem to have lower FX exposures.	*Prudence*: costs and risks in emerging markets can offset expected high returns. Test cash flows to the limit and make different scenarios.
AREAS2 (foreign exchange exposure assessed by areas related to finance): FX exposure assessed only by finance and using mostly financial tools seems to be less effective in this sample and in the region under study. Assessment by other areas (mainly marketing and operations) also seems to be less effective.	*Difficulty of origin*: emerging markets' products appear to have a perception of low-quality standardization; it also includes the low qualifications of the labour force in certain areas. This should be considered in the subsidiary's business plan, training programmes, and knowledge transfer strategies.
AUTDECISION1 (high decentralization): subsidiaries in the sample with more autonomy to make decisions related to hedging activities tend to deal better with changes in the exchange rate.	*Open eyes*: changes in demand's composition and in consumers' habits usually imply new segments and niches. Subsidiaries need autonomy to use their assets and knowledge to exploit these opportunities.

Figure 6.1 Findings from the quantitative and qualitative analyses

Finally, a recurrent comment during the interviews (and also validated by the quantitative analysis) is that hedging by financial tools is difficult (in fact, sometimes such tools are not even available) in the region under study (see sections 6.2 and 6.3.1). This outcome, along with the fact that these ten variables have an impact on the way companies internationalize their operations (mainly modes of entry, configuration of activities, and control and coordination), give extra support to the original argument of this work that a more integrated approach is needed to deal with currency fluctuations in emerging markets.

6.5 Conclusion

This chapter showed the quantitative, qualitative, and mixed method results of our study. The outcome of these analyses is that the FX exposure of the companies in the sample was impacted by ten variables. This outcome is also cross-validated and corroborated by the results obtained from the two different perspectives: quantitative and qualitative. The following chapter will present the development of a tool to minimize the FX effects on MNCs.

7
The Development of a Tool to Minimize Foreign Exchange Exposure in Emerging Markets

7.1 Introduction

This chapter presents a summary of what has been undertaken in this work, along with comments and some analysis of the findings obtained in sections 6.2, 6.3 and 6.4. It is structured as follows: the first section shows the summary mentioned before; the second section, an analysis of the results; the third section presents a framework for companies to improve the efficiency of their hedging initiatives; and, finally, the chapter concludes with recommendations, reflections, and suggestions for future research.

7.2 Summary

This section presents a summary of the quantitative and qualitative analyses resulting from survey data on the decisions and strategies against variations in the exchange rate made by a group of European companies with subsidiaries in the Mercosur region and Chile. The objective of these analyses was to examine the links between these decisions/strategies and the foreign exchange exposure of the companies in the sample (see section 4.4). Because all of these companies have international operations and actively try to hedge their exposure, the idea was to study the effectiveness of their decisions/strategies in a context of emerging countries where it is claimed that institutions, transactions costs, and resources of the firm impact companies' performance in different ways than can be expected in industrialized countries (see section 2.8). This study gains relevance in the current environment of increasing economic integration between the European Union and the Mercosur + Chile region, where the EU is the largest foreign investor.

The quantitative analysis followed the similar two-stage design used in recent literature. In the first stage, foreign exposure coefficients for each company in the sample were estimated by running a set of time series regressions (Table 6.1). In the second stage, the exposure coefficients were used as dependent variables in a cross-sectional regression on a range of independent variables which represented the data obtained in the survey about the decisions and strategies used by each company to hedge their exposures (Table 6.2). The model employed in the cross-sectional regression (Reg 4, Table 6.2) showed statistical significance, the same for the estimated coefficients.

The qualitative analysis used the data collected during the open-ended section of the interviews. The first step of this analysis involved the comparison of incidents (single phrases, sentences, or entire comments) and the generation of categories as a result. The second step implied the integration of these categories with a set of properties; and the third step the delimitation of the findings. Finally, these quantitative and qualitative analyses were integrated; they seem to cross-validate and complement each other. A discussion of the results will be presented in the next section.

7.3 Analysis of the results

The fact that a set of factors have been shown to affect the exposure of the companies in the sample, and that these factors could be attributed to different functional areas, supports the main proposition and one of the objectives of this work: a holistic approach (see Figure 3.1 and section 4.4) to hedging against fluctuations in the exchange rate is expected to contribute to reducing the impact that these variations have on the performance of companies with foreign investments in emerging markets. On the one hand, six variables from the key themes identified in the literature (Figure 4.2) have been shown to impact the value of the firms in the sample discussed above. On the other hand, this result is complemented by the conclusions of the qualitative analysis where five concepts were identified as affecting the hedging strategies of the European companies operating in the Mercosur and Chile (sections 6.2 and 6.3.8, and Figure 6.1).

An analysis of these variables/concepts within the theoretical framework presented in Chapter 4 follows.

The result of the calculations of the foreign exchange exposure is consistent with Kennedy's claim (1984) that 'foreign exchange rate always has some impact on MNCs' in the sense that all the companies in the sample showed some kind of exposure. Table 6.1 shows that the mean foreign exchange risk (β_{fx}) is 1.154, with a minimum of −4.733 and a maximum of 28.89 with a majority of statistically significant estimates, $|\beta_{fx}/S_b| > t_{n-3;0.975}$. The non-statistically significant estimates – as well as the negative ones – could be explained by the companies' hedging activities or by the offsetting impact of their operations in multiple currencies. The positive and negative signs of the exposure coefficients show the heterogeneous nature of the foreign exchange effects, consistent with the findings from recent works (Choi & Kim, 2003; Faff & Marshall, 2005). The mean of the absolute value of the foreign exchange exposure is 2.049.

The positive and negative signs of the exposure coefficients show the heterogeneous nature of the foreign exchange effects, consistent with the findings from recent works (Choi & Kim, 2003; Faff & Marshall, 2005). The country of origin as a factor playing a role in companies' exposure has been discussed in previous studies; see, for example, Hakkarainen, Joseph, Kasanen and Puttonen (1998) for Finnish companies, Choi and Kim (2003), Kennedy (1984), Miller and Reuer (1998), Noreiko and Solga (1999), Pantzalis, Simkins and Laux (2001), Shapiro (1975), and Shapiro and Rutenberg (1974) among others for US companies, Joseph and Hewins (1997) for UK companies, Oxelheim (1984) for Swedish firms, Batten, Mellor and Wan (1993) for Australian companies, Chow and Chen (1998) for Japanese firms, and Faff and Marshall (2005), who made a comparison among US, UK, and Asian Pacific companies. The findings of this work were that *ORIGIN* showed a positive relation with the foreign exchange exposure of the European companies in the sample (similar to most of the studies outside the US), providing further evidence that the results of previous research on US companies may not be applicable in all cases.

On the other hand, an analysis at the company level of Table 6.1 shows that the effectiveness of the differentiation strategy suggested by Porter (1990), Sundaram and Black (1992) and Sundaram and Mishra (1991) to hedge FX exposure is not conclusive. On the one hand, companies applying this strategy present relatively low or negative coefficients (Co1, Co4, Co20, Co22, Co25, and Co44); however, on the other hand, Co2, Co9, Co26, and Co30 show relatively high exposure to variations in the exchange rate. This conclusion is similar to that from Miller and Reuer (1998) and also to the qualitative results of this work which suggest that this strategy seems to be effective mainly when the differentiation is based on very specific knowledge/technologies.

Nevertheless, the aggregate results still suggest that the transfer of the parent's advantages strengthens the subsidiaries' ability to deal with changes in the value of currencies (*OWNERSHIP*). These results are consistent with the conclusions of earlier works (Kogut, 1983; Kogut & Kulatilaka, 1994; Miller & Reuer, 1998) in the sense that foreign direct investments help companies to reduce their foreign exchange exposure in comparison with other entry modes, such as exports or distribution contracts (Sundaram & Black, 1992).

The outcome suggesting that number of currencies (*CURRENCIES*) and number of countries (*COUNTRIES*), variables that can be interpreted as the extent of internationalization, do not present associations with the foreign exchange exposure (see section 6.2 and Table 6.2, Reg 2) differs from the findings in most of the previous works discussed throughout this volume. This difference could be explained by the fact that the measurement of the exposure is different; in this work it was measured for the country/region of origin against FX variations only in a specific region (Mercosur and Chile), when in other works it is generally gauged for the country of origin against most of the companies' international operations. Alternatively, it could imply that companies, as a result of their experience dealing with this risk, have learned how to hedge their cash flows; or because their operations in different countries help them to offset the exposure.

Other variables mentioned in the literature, and included in the model because they were identified as relevant in the context of this work (see *Figure 4.2*: Key themes), showed no associations with the foreign exchange exposure. The most notorious case is *HTUSE*, relative use of hedging tools in emerging markets, which could be explained by the findings of the qualitative analysis (see section 6.3.1) where participants recognised that financial tools to hedge foreign exchange exposure are not widely used in LA companies as most of the time they are not available in local currencies, or because their costs are higher than the [estimated] potential risks. Funding in local currency also seems difficult to obtain as banks (and local financial markets) do not have the capacity to finance large projects in currencies from emerging countries and because the uncertainties of these countries make financial institutions ask for relatively short repayment periods. Previous works (see, for example, Chow et al., 1997a, 1997b; Martin & Mauer, 2003; Pringle, 1991; Pringle & Connolly, 1993) also claimed that it is unclear whether financial hedging is useful (although their conclusions were obtained in different geographical contexts).

Another key theme suggested by the literature (see, for example, Miller & Reuer, 1998) as relevant for hedging where no association with foreign exchange exposure was found is the stage when the company considers economic exposure when investing abroad (planning stage or when the subsidiary is already operating), represented by *STAGE2* in the model (sections 5.6.1 and 6.2). This result could have its origins in a number of potentially interrelated elements. In terms of the data, one explanation could be that the majority of the companies in the sample made their first (and largest) investment in the region many years before this study (mainly over five) and now their cash flows seem to be hedged, at least to a certain extent. This situation could have provided the study with biased answers as participants are not planning new investments and therefore they do not see the need to design new hedging strategies.

The relations and contributions between the variables-concepts found to have a potential impact on companies' exposure (Figure 6.1) and the research perspectives presented in section 2.8 can be seen below:

a. *Institutional theory*: studies using this theory in emerging markets have shown that institutions affect the performance of organizations in both positive and negative ways. The findings of this work present similar conclusions; the great majority of the companies in the sample claimed that institutions impact upon and have impacted upon their profitability in a negative way. The areas identified as responsible for this impact were: (i) the low independence from political power; (ii) the difficulty of controlling the shadow economy that presents opportunities to unfair competition; (iii) the continuous changes in government officials that make negotiations with governments more difficult; and (iv) the quality of the regulators (sections 6.3.3 and 6.3.8).

b. *Transaction costs economics*: one of the areas identified by previous works using this theory states that transaction costs in emerging markets are higher than those in developed economies (point b, section 2.8). The first reason given for this is that the price system does not give reliable information for the efficient allocation of resources and, as a consequence, the measurement of costs tends to be higher. The following findings from this work fall within this framework: (i) governments' interventions in the foreign exchange market give a false sense of international competitiveness; (ii) fluctuations in the exchange rate are a hurdle to the definition of plans, budgets, standards, and control systems as well as the design of the supply chain; (iii) extra money [hidden costs] is needed to raise the productivity, quality standards, and training; and (iv) hedging tools are relatively more expensive and not widely available (sections 6.3.1, 6.3.2, and 6.3.5). The second reason given by previous studies for higher transactions costs in emerging markets is the government's discretion rather than the rule of law; evidence of this was also found in the dispute over prices in the privatised utility companies in Argentina (sections 6.3.2 and 6.3.8).
c. *Resource-based view of the firm*: the application of this theory in emerging markets suggests that the development of value-creating assets is difficult and most of the time implies the establishment of good relationships with local government (point c, section 2.8). The results of this work tend to corroborate this; close relations with local governments (in the form of local partners and/or local managers) was identified as a key factor when dealing with regulators and/or negotiating the price of public services (section 6.3.4). In addition, this work provides contributions in this area in emerging markets as evidence was found which suggested that: (i) the transfer of the parent's advantages strengthens the subsidiaries' position to deal with changes in the value of different currencies (as suggested by variable *OWNERSHIP* structure, section 6.2); and (ii) the high decentralization/more autonomy given to subsidiaries to make decisions on hedging initiatives seems to be more effective in dealing with the effects of (unexpected and/or high) variations in the exchange rate (*AUTDECISION1*, section 6.2), especially by allowing subsidiaries to use their assets and knowledge to exploit

new segments and niches as a consequence of unanticipated (and important) changes in the composition of demand and consumer's habits (*Open Eyes*, section 6.3.8).

As stated at the beginning of this section, the fact that several factors that can be attributed to different functional areas have proved to have an impact upon companies' performances in emerging markets gives support to the holistic approach proposed as the first objective of this work. Similar findings have been presented in previous works (see, for example, Aggarwal & Soenen, 1989); however, these have been studied in the context of developed economies. This is one of the main differences, and at the same time a contribution of this work, as studies in this field in emerging countries are scarce. Another contribution is that the findings are based on empirical data gathered from a survey in the form of interviews with senior managers/directors of companies exposed to the phenomenon under study; this data collection method also offered the possibility to analyse qualitative data as well as to get an in-depth understanding of the issue from the companies' perspective. Finally, the Europe-wide sample (which represents over 50 per cent of the funds invested in the emerging region under study) offers a broader perspective than previous works based mainly on the US and/or referred to single countries of origin.

7.4 How can companies benefit from this work?

From the outset, this work aimed to offer alternatives to hedging for companies with subsidiaries in emerging countries. This is the main reason behind the second objective of this work – the development of a framework to help companies to improve the effectiveness of their hedging activities in emerging markets. The development of this framework is based on the Matrix of Multiple Sources of Authority and Denominations of Value proposed by Sundaram and Black (1992) and explained in section 4.1.2. Their work was developed more than 15 years ago when emerging markets were less integrated into the world's economy in terms of trade and investments, as is shown by current figures; consequently, it is possible to assume that this matrix refers mainly to MNCs from Triad countries with investments and/or operations in developed nations.

As presented in Chapter 2 and in section 5.4, emerging countries are becoming increasingly integrated into the world's economy and companies from Triad countries are investing in these countries searching for resources and/or markets. From the findings of this work (presented in sections 6.2 and 6.3) the management of subsidiaries in emerging markets seems to be slightly different from the practices generally used in Triad countries. This was also corroborated in points a, b, and c of section 7.3. For these reasons, and in order to provide alternatives for companies, it was deemed necessary to use the existing knowledge to adapt existing techniques and/or develop new frameworks to be applied in the context of emerging markets.

It is within this framework that the aim of this section will be to complement and adapt Sundaram and Black's proposition in the context of emerging markets, specifically to the region under study. The matrix can be seen in Figure 7.1; the upper box on the right-hand side (with grey background) representing high MV and high MA will be the main object of the present analysis. In the original work, high MV and MA meant a large number of different currencies and a large number of different authorities to deal with. In the context of this work it will be assumed: (i) that MNCs first invested in industrialized countries and then went to emerging markets, totalling a relatively 'high' number of currencies and authorities (like the case of most of the companies in the sample); and (ii) that high MV and MA also include the possibility of high variations in the value of currencies and the volatility in the institutions, like the situation observed in the emerging countries, which are the focus of this study.

Using the ten variables-concepts that were shown to have a potential impact on the firms' value as a consequence of fluctuations in the exchange rate (Figure 6.1), it would be possible to apply a holistic approach formed by these variables-concepts in the High MA and MV box. Entry Mode and Strategy fall within the analysis of Strategic Planning (section 3.3.4), Configuration within Operations Management and Marketing (the latter mainly pricing and product, sections 3.3.3 and 3.3.2) and Control within Finance (section 3.3.1). The outcomes of this application can be seen below in Figure 7.2.

Figure 7.2 presents the application of Sundaram and Black's model to the context of emerging markets using the findings obtained in this work, based upon quantitative and qualitative analyses of the data collected in a survey conducted with senior managers/directors

MA					
MA	High	Entry:	Primarily export, some contract, low FDI	Entry:	Primarily contract, some export, low FDI
		Configuration:	Primarily concentrated and undifferentiated	Configuration:	Primarily dispersed and undifferentiated
		Control:	Primarily formalisation, some socialization, low centralization	Control:	Primarily socialization, low formalization, low centralization
		Strategy:	Value-based and some value/cost-based strategies	Strategy:	Value-based strategies
	Low	Entry:	Primarily export, some contract, low FDI	Entry:	Primarily FDI, some contract, low export
		Configuration:	Primarily concentrated and differentiated	Configuration:	Primarily dispersed and differentiated
		Control:	Primarily centralization, some formalization, low socialization	Control:	Primarily formalization, some socialization, low centralization
		Strategy:	Primarily cost-based strategies	Strategy:	Primarily value-based strategies
		Low		High	
		MV			

Figure 7.1 Matrix of Multiple Sources of Authority (MA) and Denominations of Value (MV)
Source: Sundaram and Black (1992).

Entry mode	Primarily FDI with majority control to transfer the parent's advantages without risking proprietary assets due to governments' discretion in the enforcement of property rights legislation.
Configuration of activities	Primarily dispersed (to take advantage of the cost differences where the MNC operates), differentiated (to be able to develop products tailored to the local market), and flexible (to adapt easily to changes in the environment as well as to exploit the new segments and niches formed as a consequence of these changes).
Control	Primarily formalization (in the form of the development of an exchange rate policy along with the assessment of FX exposure by finance and other related areas, and close monitoring of the progress of strategic plans), decentralization to make decisions related to hedging activities, and some socialization mainly in the work with local managers and/or local partners (to provide local knowledge and manage the relations with the local government).
Strategy	Primarily value-based strategies (only when the advantage is based on a very specific technology/knowledge and considering a potential difficulty when planning exports from the host country due to a perception of low quality).

Figure 7.2 Application of a holistic approach for protecting a firm's value against variations in the FX in emerging markets

of European companies with subsidiaries in selected Latin American countries. As can be seen, four functional areas are represented, reflecting the idea that a holistic approach is needed to improve the effectiveness of the management of foreign exchange exposure in emerging markets. In addition, this framework is intended to offer companies alternatives when operating in these markets, achieving, thus, the second objective of this work.

The holistic approach could also be seen as a cross-functional or multi-functional strategy. The literature, and also the companies in the sample, have been tackling hedging mainly from the perspective of a centralized and finance-only responsibility. However, the findings from this empirical work present hedging in emerging markets as a responsibility of the different areas within the organization, with subsidiaries receiving enough autonomy to make decisions to protect their foreign exchange exposure. This idea can be seen using the same format presented at the beginning of Chapter 3; Figure 7.3 shows an adaptation of Figure 3.1 using the results of this work.

The results of this work show: (i) that FDI and value-based strategies can be effective in minimizing some of the effects of currency crises; (ii) that unanticipated fluctuations in the value of currencies in

Figure 7.3 A holistic approach to hedging against fluctuations in the exchange rate

emerging markets affect different areas within the company and that an effective way to deal with this challenge is by assessing the foreign exchange exposure among the different functional areas; and (iii) that giving more autonomy to subsidiaries operating in changing environments to make decisions and implement initiatives against foreign exchange exposure seems to be effective in dealing with this risk.

In conclusion, from this empirical work it is possible to conclude that a pre-emptive and cross-functional approach is needed to protect the company's value against variations in emerging countries' exchange rates; i.e., hedging in emerging markets seems to imply more than protecting cash flows with financial instruments.

7.5 Suggestions for future research

These results provide a basis for future research into the effects of unanticipated variations in the exchange rate on companies with investments in emerging markets. Because of the current trends of investments in these countries/regions and increasing economic integration, it would be worthwhile studying European companies' investments (or those of companies from other industrialized countries) in other emerging markets (such as Eastern Europe or Asia Pacific). It would also be worthwhile to compare the findings of this study, analysing the international cash flow structures of companies operating in emerging markets as positive (negative) variations in production costs due to changes in the exchange rate could be offset by positive (negative) effects on income. It can also be interesting to study how SMEs' operations in emerging countries are affected by large and unexpected changes in the value of local currencies.

On the other hand, Figures 7.2 and 7.3 show how a cross/multi-functional approach can be applied to the context of management in emerging markets, specifically to hedging against exchange rate variations. This framework was developed as a result of the study of European companies' subsidiaries in the Mercosur region and Chile and is expected to be a motivation for future research. One area of future interest would be an analysis of regional differences – that is, companies from other Triad countries with investments in (the same or other) emerging region/s. A second area of interest for future research implies a change in the perspective; most of the works in this field take the position of companies from industrialized countries with investments/subsidiaries in emerging markets and how the parent companies hedge the value of their operations. The new perspective would take the view of the subsidiaries, especially considering the current context of the increasing importance of emerging markets in the MNCs' value chains, the findings suggesting decentralization of their hedging decisions, as well as the increasing relative weight of subsidiaries from emerging markets in the whole structure of the MNCs. The latter can be seen in the relative size/weight that subsidiaries operating in China are reaching, a situation that will probably be seen in the future in India and other large emerging countries, such as Russia and Brazil.

7.6 Some concluding remarks

As is the case with much research, this work has followed the logic of positivism; a clear theoretical framework and a proved methodology. Nevertheless, and as the results of the exploratory nature of the qualitative analysis, some interesting topics arose. These topics have not been widely studied within the original conceptual framework of hedging against currency fluctuations; however, this section seems to provide a good opportunity to mention them, especially in the context of the holistic approach to management discussed in previous sections and chapters.

The first – and most commonly mentioned – issue was that of the cost of the currency crises for the persons within the organizations. Participants talked mainly about two problems: (i) that of the executives making hard decisions (and sometimes with little strategic support) under conditions of extreme uncertainty in very short periods of time, such as sudden lay-offs, delays in the payment of wages due to cash flow restrictions, default on the company's financial obligations (sometimes breaking long-standing commercial relations and/or personal promises), heated discussions with the parent, long working hours to solve the endless problems, among others; and (ii) that of the employees suffering the consequences of these 'rushed' decisions, who did not always understand the rationale behind them. Interviewees agreed that this situation impacted the company's culture and morale, and that many people paid a high cost. Examples of this cost were the increased number of accidents, health problems, dissatisfaction, lack of interest, stress, and the loss of personnel to the competitors.

Secondly, participants also highlighted the differences in the management of organizations in emerging countries. These differences were seen in the 'expats' working in South America, as well as in the local people trying to internalize the (relatively) higher standards of MNCs. This issue appears as a potential source for future research in the areas of training, knowledge management, and MNC–subsidiary relations.

Third is the difficulty of designing the supply chain because of the changing nature of the environment. This issue falls within the operational hedging mentioned in the literature; however, there are some issues that companies still need to resolve as they need to keep their operations up and running regardless of the problems created by currency crises. For example, most of these European companies designed their operations based on the incentives offered by each host country, but the changing business environment acts as a threat to the design of an operational hedging, a disincentive to expand the local operations, and a source of uncertainty that prevents embarking on new local developments. In this context, it is worth mentioning the comment from one of the interviewees that the economic integration between developing countries potentially increases the 'shock wave' of the currency crises, making the situation even more difficult to manage. These are revealing comments that have not always been considered by the literature on international business, international management, or economic integration.

Finally, management is a broad discipline that has relations with many other areas, including, among others, economics, politics, engineering and sociology. This broad approach was attempted in this research by including inputs from different subjects and, by doing so, it was expected that the findings would be relevant to this broad field of management. In particular, one of the most renowned theories in the internationalization of business (Buckley & Casson, 1976) claims that multinational firms are able to reduce transaction costs by internalizing product markets as well as to increase value added in a cost-effective way by establishing overseas operations. In this context, this work intends to make a contribution in the area of transactions costs in companies' operations in emerging markets by helping them to reduce their exchange risk exposure. In addition, it attempts to build a bridge between theory and practice.

8

An Example of the Use of the Tool

8.1 Introduction

This chapter will give an example of the use of the tool presented in Chapter 7 to seven companies from a developed country with investments in emerging markets. In order to do this, it will first obtain the foreign exchange exposure coefficient of these companies. Then it will show information collected about the decisions and strategies taken by these firms to minimize the foreign exchange exposure before and during a period of high turbulence in the currency markets. Finally, the two sets of results will be compared and conclusions will be made.

8.2 Foreign exchange exposure coefficient calculation

Our analysis was carried out in a similar way to that shown in section 5.6.1. The election of this model was based on: (i) the possibility of assessing the overall impact of changes in the currency price on the value of the firm; (ii) its flexibility; and (iii) its forward-looking nature (a discussion of its weaknesses can be found in section 3.4).

A coefficient of foreign exchange exposure of the companies in the sample was calculated through a time series regression of the companies' stock returns on market and foreign exchange returns. In a similar manner to section 5.6.1, foreign exchange risk was defined as changes in the value of the firm as a consequence of changes in the value of the currency. The calculations used contemporaneous exchange rates. The equation can be seen below:

$$R_{it} = a + \beta_m R_{mt} + \beta_{fx} R_{fxt} + \varepsilon_{it} \quad (4)$$

Table 8.1 Operating profits by origin, 2000 and 2003

		CoO	EM1	EM2	EM3	EM4	EM5	EM6	EM7	RoW
Co1	**2000**	84.0%	5.0%	1.6%	2.2%		3.5%		2.7%	0.8%
	2003	58.2%	0.0%	0.0%	1.7%		28.7%		6.2%	5.2%
Co2	**2000**	60.5%	9.8%	7.4%	10.1%	6.3%		5.9%		0.0%
	2003	59.6%	3.3%	10.7%	12.0%	5.0%		4.8%		4.6%
Co3	**2000**	74.0%	14.9%	4.3%		1.3%	5.5%			0.0%
	2003	87.3%	3.3%	2.0%		3.0%	4.2%			0.7%
Co4	**2000**	95.1%	2.4%				1.6%			0.5%
	2003	91.5%	4.6%				3.4%			0.5%
Co5	**2000**	34.7%	45.3%							20.0%
	2003	21.2%	56.9%							21.9%
Co6	**2000**	58.1%	7.5%	8.6%	8.9%		8.9%		3.7%	4.7%
	2003	63.8%	0.0%	15.9%	5.5%		9.2%		2.4%	3.3%
Co7	**2000**	56.0%	12.0%	21.0%	5.0%			5.0%		1.0%
	2003	69.6%	4.3%	17.8%	4.9%			4.2%		−0.8%

Source: Companies' annual reports 1998–2003.

where R_{it} is the return of company i in period t, R_{mt} is the return for the market index in period t, and R_{fxt} is the return on real exchange rate in period t weighted by the country of origin of the EBITDA for each company. An example of each company's situation for two years can be seen in Table 8.1. This table shows the origin of the EBITDA in 2000 and 2003 for seven companies (Co1, Co2, etc) from eight specific countries and also from the rest of the companies' international operations; the first column on the left presents the EBITDA from the Country of Origin (CoO) and then the operating profits generated in seven emerging markets (EM1, EM2, etc.). The last column on the right shows the percentage for the rest of the world (RoW).

Monthly data from 1 January 1998 to 31 December 2004, a period that was characterized by crises in most of the emerging countries' currencies, were used in the calculations.[1] The outcomes can be seen in Table 8.2, which shows the estimates for market risk and foreign exchange exposure. This coefficient shows the sensitivity of the companies' value to changes in the exchange rate of the countries under study using the return on market index (the principal stock index of the country of origin) as statistical control.[2] Only one country

Table 8.2 Estimates for market risk and foreign exchange exposure, t statistics in italics

	β_m	β_{fx}
Co 1	0.00	−0.01
t	*7.42*	*−0.55*
Co 2	0.00	−0.06
t	*9.93*	*−2.08*
Co 3	0.00	−0.20
t	*4.95*	*−2.46*
Co 4	0.00	0.14
t	*1.20*	*4.50*
Co 5	0.00	0.02
t	*8.60*	*2.26*
Co 6	0.00	0.03
t	*12.13*	*2.70*
Co 7	0.00	0.13
t	*11.10*	*3.25*
Mean	**0.00**	**0.01**
|Mean|	**0.00**	**0.08**
Min	**0.00**	**−0.20**
Max	**0.00**	**0.14**
Positive	7	**4**

of origin was used in this exercise to provide a common source of reporting and accounting rules and therefore to give coherence to the information.[3]

In Table 8.2, it is possible to see that the mean market risk (β_m) across the sample is 0.00; this may be explained by the high weight of these companies in the market index used as statistical control. All the companies have a positive beta estimate, and the vast majority of these positive betas are statistically significant ($|\beta_m/S_b| > t_{n-3;\ 0.975}$). It is also possible to see that the mean foreign exchange risk (β_{fx}) is 0.01, with a minimum of −0.20 and a maximum of 0.14. In this case, the majority of these estimates are statistically significant ($|\beta_{fx}/S_b| > t_{n-3;\ 0.975}$). This was expected as the companies in the sample had foreign exchange exposure due to their operations overseas (see Table 8.1). The non-statistically significant estimates as well as the negative ones could be explained by the companies' hedging activities or the offsetting impact of their operations in multiple currencies. The mean of the absolute value of the foreign exchange exposure is 0.08.

In Table 8.1 the analysis of each company's situation shows three tiers of foreign exchange exposure: low (Co1), medium (Co2, Co5, and Co6), and high (Co3, Co4, and Co7). Co3, Co4, and Co7 present the relatively highest exposure, meaning that for every 1 per cent movement in the weighted exchange rate index for each company, the value of these three companies have been affected by around –20 per cent, 14 per cent, and 13 per cent respectively (controlling for independent variables in the equation).

The medium and high tiers imply some (medium or high) impact on the value of these companies as the variations in the price of the emerging countries' currencies during the period under study have shown responsibility in the changes in the price of these firms' shares. It is also possible to say that this impact has been negative in the sense that these companies were not successful in convincing the market of the strength of their hedging strategies. The latter is relevant in the context of this exercise as the seven companies said that they were using some kind of financial hedging instrument to protect the value of their investments in the emerging markets under study.[4]

8.3 Hedging activities

The seven companies recognised that both the extent and the consequences of the currency crises in these emerging countries were difficult to anticipate. The result was that both the performance and the daily operations of their subsidiaries operating in these countries were affected in many different ways; even in the case of those overseas operations hedged with financial instruments.

They also said that they have applied non-financial mechanisms to protect the value of their investments in emerging markets. All of them employed a policy of majority control in their foreign investments with the aim of transferring the parent's firm-specific advantages to the subsidiaries (a strategy identified as effective in hedging against foreign exchange exposure; see section 3.3.4 for more details). But as this majority control was mainly a 'knowledge transfer' strategy rather than a hedging strategy, it is not considered a pre-emptive hedging measure within the context of this study.

Companies also said that, in general, before/during the crises they did not implement initiatives in areas other than finance (for example, marketing, operations management, strategic planning, and so on) aimed specifically at protecting the value of their investments overseas.

After the main period of high volatility in the value of the currencies, and as a consequence of its impact on the companies' operations and cash flow, companies designed complex tools, policies, and mechanisms to protect their cash flows from unexpected variations in the exchange rate. For example, they created dedicated teams based in the HQ that constantly monitor the economic, financial, and political situation in the host countries. These teams now report to the highest level of the company at short intervals (for example, every 15 days in one of the cases) and have a direct link to the subsidiaries' commercial policy. The majority of these companies also developed exchange rate policies.

As can be seen, these companies based their original hedging strategies on financial tools and this may be one of the reasons for the impact on the companies' value presented in Table 8.2. But then they seem to have recognised that these tools were not completely effective in dealing with the currency crises in these emerging markets. As a consequence, they started the development and use of post-crises, cross-functional initiatives to protect their overseas investments against foreign exchange exposure.

These initiatives started as the unexpected fluctuations in the value of the currencies of these emerging markets impacted their cash flows and also because financial hedging 'is not enough', as one of them put it. The companies added that these cross-functional initiatives have helped them to have a better understanding and a closer look at the environment of these emerging markets.

However, these seem to be reactive strategies; no currency crises have occurred since their implementation to measure the results, and they could eventually magnify the consequences of a crisis if the decisions taken are short-sighted ones. Finally, this also shows the indirect effects of the foreign exchange exposure, its longer-term nature, and again raises questions over the effectiveness of financial hedging in emerging markets.

8.4 Foreign exchange exposure versus hedging activities

An analysis of the three tiers of foreign exchange exposure (described previously) against the information collected from the companies was carried out with the aim of assessing the effectiveness of their hedging strategies. This analysis looked at the relations, differences, and similarities in the hedging strategies pursued by the companies in the different tiers.

First, companies in the high exposure tier (Co3, Co4, and Co7) are the ones with the relatively lower operating profit coming from the seven emerging markets in 2003 (see Table 8.1). This can be explained by a possible offsetting effect of the operations in multiple currencies of the companies in the other two tiers.

Secondly, Co3 and Co7 saw an important reduction in the operating profits produced in the emerging markets under study between 2000 and 2003 (Table 8.1); companies said that this reduction was a consequence of unanticipated variations in the cash flow, decreases in the demand for their products, changes in the composition of the demand, debtors in arrears, non-performing debts, and changes in the supply chain, and that the financial hedging was not effective. In addition, the three companies in the high exposure tier recognised that their foreign exchange risk assessment was carried out only by the finance area. These findings provide extra evidence of the indirect and longer-term effects of the variations in the exchange rate and also why financial hedging instruments are not always effective. They also lend support to the idea that a cross-functional approach to hedging foreign exchange exposure may offer a more effective way to deal with this risk.

Finally, the six companies in the high and medium exposure tiers said that the subsidiaries' degree of autonomy to make decisions and implement initiatives against foreign exchange risk is medium and low (contrary to what was suggested by Sundaram and Black (1992), see Figure 7.1). Co1, the only one with low exposure, has given high autonomy to the regional headquarters located in EM5.

In summary, from this information and also using the figures from the firms' balance sheets, it would be possible to say that: (i) companies with operations in multiple currencies have higher possibilities of offsetting their foreign exchange exposure; (ii) unexpected fluctuations in the value of the currencies in emerging markets affect different areas within the company and that an effective way to deal with this challenge is by assessing the foreign exchange exposure among the different functional areas; and (iii) giving more autonomy to subsidiaries operating in changing environments to make decisions and implement initiatives against foreign exchange exposure seems to be effective in dealing with this risk.

8.5 Conclusions

This chapter has given a brief illustration of how the model presented in this book can be used in practice. It analysed the annual reports and qualitative information on the decisions and strategies aimed at protecting the value of companies against variations in the exchange rate made by seven companies with operations in emerging markets. The objective of this analysis was to examine the links between these decisions/strategies and the foreign exchange exposure of the companies. These firms have international operations and actively try to hedge their exposure.

In section 8.2, a foreign exchange exposure coefficient for each company was estimated by running a set of time series regressions. Following this, in section 8.3 a description of the companies' hedging initiatives was given. These firms principally made use of financial hedging instruments before/during the crises. Then, and likely as a consequence of a learning process, they developed and adopted models to manage exchange risk and mitigate impacts based on the active participation of the different functional areas in the companies.

Finally, these two analyses were integrated with the aim of analysing the effectiveness of the decisions considering the foreign exchange exposure coefficient obtained in the first step. The analysis showed that: (i) companies with operations in multiple currencies have higher possibilities of offsetting their foreign exchange exposure; (ii) unexpected fluctuations in the value of the currencies in emerging markets affect different areas within the company and that an effective way to deal with this challenge is by assessing the foreign exchange exposure between the functional areas; and (iii) giving more autonomy to subsidiaries operating in changing environments to make decisions and implement initiatives against foreign exchange exposure seems to be effective in dealing with this risk. Taken together, these are similar conclusions to those obtained in Chapter 7 and explained in Figure 7.3.

Appendix 1: Theoretical Framework of the Methodology

A1.1 Introduction

This appendix presents the theoretical framework of the methodology used in this research work. It begins with a short discussion of the different research philosophies; there then follows an analysis of different sample techniques; thirdly, the text continues to study the data collection techniques; and fourthly, this section presents an explanation of the data analysis tools employed. Chapter 5 looks at how these assumptions, tools, and techniques were used in the context of this work.

A1.2 Research philosophy

The philosophy behind a research work represents the main framework within which that work will be developed. The decision about this philosophy depends mainly upon how the researcher sees the development of knowledge. In order to assist with this decision, Easterby-Smith, Thorpe, and Lowe (2002) presented the perspectives that dominate the literature – positivism and Social constructionism – along with their implications in Table A1.1.

Once the philosophy has been decided, the researcher needs to choose which research approach to take; deductive, 'in which you [the researcher] develop a theory and hypotheses and design a research strategy to test the hypothesis', or inductive, 'in which you [the researcher] would collect data and develop theory as a result of your [the researcher's] data analysis' (Saunders et al., 2003). Attempting to attach these approaches to one of the two perspectives presented in Table A1.1 could be confusing and may be of no value; however, it could be said that the deductive approach is closer to positivism and that the inductive approach closer to Social constructionism.

The first approach, deduction or theory testing, is mainly used when 'laws provide the basis of explanation, permit the anticipation of phenomena, predict their occurrence and therefore allow

Table A1.1 Main development of knowledge perspectives

		Positivism	Social constructionism
1	The observer	Must be independent	Is part of what is being observed
2	Human interests	Should be irrelevant	Are the main drivers of science
3	Explanations	Must demonstrate causality	Aim to increase general understanding of the situation
4	Research progresses through	Hypotheses and deductions	Gathering rich data from which ideas are induced
5	Concepts	Need to be operationalized so that they can be measured	Should incorporate stakeholder perspectives
6	Units of analysis	Should be reduced to simplest terms	May include the complexity of 'whole' situations
7	Generalization through	Statistical probability	Theoretical abstraction
8	Sampling requires	Large numbers selected randomly	Small numbers of cases chosen for specific reasons

Source: Easterby-Smith et al. (2002).

them to be controlled' (Hussey & Hussey, 1997). In this context, one important characteristic of the deductive approach is the search for the explanation of causal relationships between variables. Another characteristic is the collection of quantitative data to test a set of hypotheses, and, third, this test is usually carried out in controlled environments so the results are based on what is being measured rather than on external effects. Fourth, the research follows a highly structured methodology in order to help replication (Gill & Johnson, 1997) and ensure reliability. Fifth, the researcher in deductive studies is independent of what is being analysed. Sixth, the concepts need to be operationalized in order to enable a quantitative measurement of facts and events. Finally, deduction is characterized by the possibility of generalization through the selection of a sample of a sufficient numerical size.

In the second approach, induction or theory building, 'theory would follow data rather than vice versa as in the deductive approach'. One of the strengths of the inductive approach is that it allows an understanding of the way 'in which humans interpreted their social world' (Saunders et al., 2003). Another strength of induction is its flexibility to reveal alternative explanations of the phenomenon under study, especially in comparison with a rigid methodology in the deductive approach. Third, theory building pays important consideration to the context in which the events take place. Finally, researchers following this approach tend to use different methods to collect mainly qualitative data from smaller samples (than in deductive works).

A1.3 Research designs

The research design describes the vehicle used to carry out a research project. Saunders, Lewis and Thornhill (2003) present the most commonly used:

- Experiment,
- Survey,
- Case study,
- Grounded theory,
- Ethnography,
- Action research,
- Cross-sectional and longitudinal studies,
- Exploratory, descriptive and explanatory studies.

The design used in a research project is closely linked to the philosophy selected for the work. In this context, Easterby-Smith et al. (2002) showed the relative position of each research design in relation to its closeness to the research philosophies mentioned above in Table A1.1 as well as to the position of the observer. These positions can be seen in Figure A1.1.

A1.3.1 Survey

Survey studies are usually linked to the positivist philosophy, as can be seen in Figure A1.1. In this context, surveys can take two different forms: (i) cross-sectional, when the study intends to analyse a set

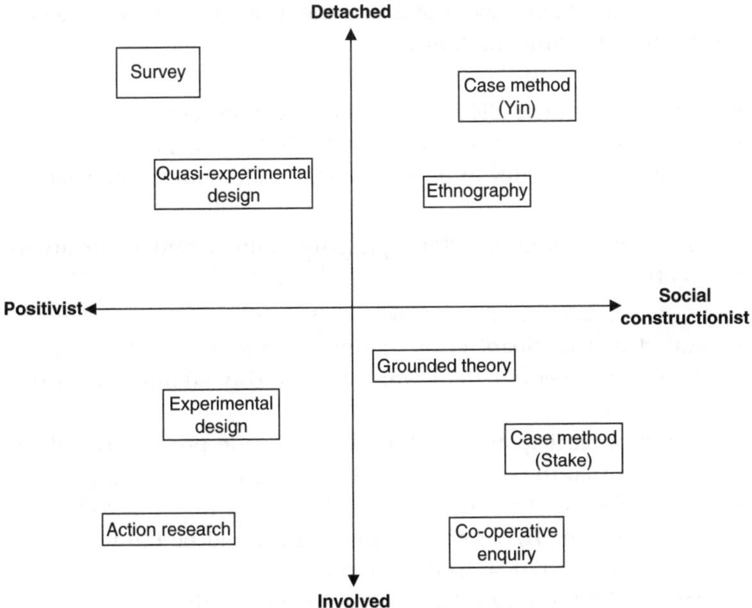

Figure A1.1 Research designs in relation to the research philosophies and the position of the observer
Source: Easterby-Smith et al. (2002).

of events at a particular time; and (ii) longitudinal, when the study is carried out over time. This type of study usually employs questionnaires to collect data; but it is also commonly seen in the use of structured observations or structured interviews. Surveys are popular as they present an efficient alternative to collecting standardized data from large populations giving, thus, the possibility of easy comparisons. However, the scope of surveys is limited to the number of questions that can be included in a questionnaire/interview as well as in the number of questionnaires/interviews that can be carried out in a certain period (Saunders et al., 2003).

A1.4 Soundness of research conclusions

The soundness of the research conclusions are based mainly on the research design and it is usually assessed by its reliability and validity.

Easterby-Smith et al. (2002) said that the reliability can be tested by asking the following questions:

- 'Will the measures yield the same results on other occasions?
- Will similar observations be reached by other observers?
- Is there transparency in how sense was made from the raw data?'

In this context, Robson (2002) presented four potential threats to reliability:

- Subject or participant error: the measurement should be carried out within a 'neutral' framework in order to avoid influences from external sources;
- Subject or participant bias: the data collection process should try to ensure that the respondents are answering what is being asked;
- Observer error: this threat is usually seen when the collection of data is done by different persons and could be minimized by increasing the standardization of the process;
- Observer bias: it means that the subjectivity of the observer could be passed to the data collected.

On the other hand, validity 'is concerned with whether the findings are really about what they appear to be about' (Saunders et al., 2003). Robson (2002) showed the potential threats to the validity of a set of research conclusions:

- *History*: events happening before the observations could influence the outcome of the data collection process,
- *Testing*: it could happen when the data collection method affects the behaviour of the event,
- *Instrumentation*: when the application of the test influences the answers from respondents,
- *Mortality*: can be found when participants drop out from a study,
- *Maturation*: when events that happen over time have an effect on the observations,
- *Ambiguity about causal direction*: in some studies, it could be difficult to state the direction of the causal relationship between two variables.

A third test for the soundness of a set of research conclusions is its generalizability or external validity. This test attempts to see the extent to which these conclusions can be applied to a different research setting.

A1.5 Selecting a sample

'Sampling techniques provide a range of methods that enable you [the researcher] to reduce the amount of data you need to collect by considering only data from a subgroup rather than all possible cases or elements' (Saunders et al., 2003). These sampling techniques offer a good option when it is not possible to survey the complete population, or when budgetary or time restrictions do not allow for a survey of the entire population. The sampling techniques can be divided into two areas: probability or representative sampling, and non-probability or judgemental sampling. The difference between them is that with representative samples the probability of each observation being selected is known and equal in all cases; therefore, this technique is used in research works requiring statistical estimations of the characteristics of the population from the observations in the sample. On the other hand, non-probabilistic samples do not allow the making of statistical inferences about the attributes of the population; for this reason, the generalization cannot be based upon statistical grounds. The selection of the sample technique depends upon the characteristics of the study, the budgetary and time restrictions, and the attributes of the population, among other things. Saunders, Lewis, and Thornhill presented the different sampling techniques in Figure A1.2.

A1.6 Data collection

Interviews are a powerful method of collecting data for a research work that are usually categorized as structured, semi-structured, or unstructured. The first type, the structured interview, is characterized by the use of predetermined and standardized questions; the second type, semi-structured, contain different topics, themes, and questions to be covered by the researcher, but these could differ from interview to interview. The differences could be in the order of the questions, the emphasis on a particular issue, or even the omission of a topic in a specific context. The third type, unstructured interviews, includes

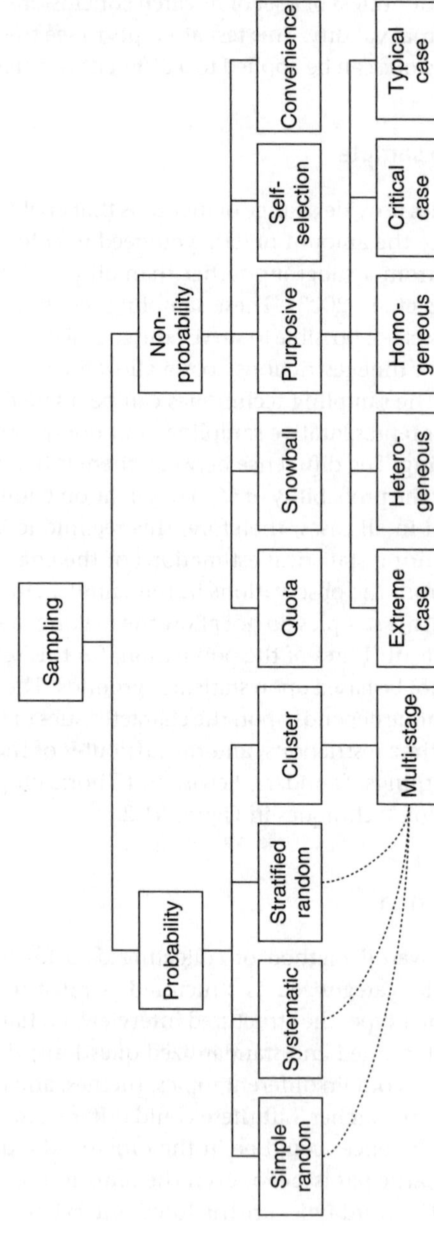

Figure A1.2 Sampling technique
Source: Saunders et al. (2003).

Table A1.2 Applications of the different types of interviews

	Exploratory	**Descriptive**	**Explanatory**
Structured		More Frequent	Less Frequent
Semi-structured	Less Frequent		More Frequent
Unstructured	More Frequent		

Source: Adapted from Saunders et al. (2003).

those where the researcher has clear ideas to discuss throughout the meeting but without any order or any specific question, and most of the time the interviewee can talk freely about the issues under study.

These types of interviews serve different purposes. For example, structured interviews are useful for quantitative analysis; by contrast, semi-structured and unstructured interviews are mainly used in qualitative studies. Saunders, Lewis and Thornhill (2003) summarized the different types of interviews and their applications in Table A1.2.

A1.7 Data analysis

As mentioned in previous sections, the data collected could be analysed using either quantitative or qualitative approaches. The range in each case varies greatly; for this reason, the next sub-section (A1.7.1) will focus on regression analysis (a widely used data analysis technique for quantitative data in social sciences) and the following sub-section A1.7.2 on the analysis of qualitative data. Finally, sub-section A1.7.3 will show how these two approaches are used together.

A1.7.1 Regression analysis (quantitative data)

Regression analysis can be found in research works that enquire about the relationship between two or more variables. In its simplest form, this relationship can be expressed by the following equation:

$$\mathrm{Y_i} = a + b\,\mathrm{X_i} \qquad (5)$$

where X represents the independent variable (the cause), Y the dependent variable (the effect), and the coefficients *a* and *b* the height and

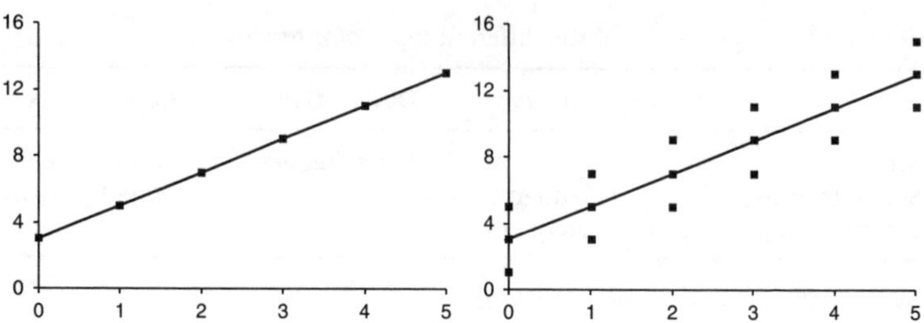

Figure A1.3 Examples of exact and inexact relationships between two variables

steepness of the line. Coefficient *a* is generally referred to as the intercept or constant and coefficient *b* as the slope. Equation 4 presents the formula for a straight line, which means that the relationship between X and Y is an exact one; this kind of relation is usually found in physics, for example. However, in social sciences the relationship between variables is usually inexact. For this reason, the formula used for a linear relationship between two social science variables would be written as:

$$Y_i = a + b X_i + e_i \tag{6}$$

where *e* represents the presence of error. 'The error term acknowledges that the prediction equation by itself ($Y = a + bX$), does not perfectly predict Y' (Lewis-Beck, 1993). The difference between exact and inexact linear relationships can be seen in Figure A1.3. The left-hand chart shows an exact linear relationship while the chart on the right presents an inexact linear relationship.

The differences mentioned above are based mainly on the fact that social sciences researchers usually assume linearity – an assumption that is not always true. Nevertheless, Lewis-Beck (1993) says that this assumption has been a starting point for many research works based on the following:

- 'Numerous relationships have been found empirically to be linear,
- The linear specification is generally the most parsimonious,
- Our [social science] theory is often so weak that we are not at all sure what the non-linear specification would be,

- Inspection of the data themselves may fail to suggest a clear alternative to the straight line model.'

In this context, social researchers should always take into consideration the possibility that the relationship was non-linear. In these cases, as mentioned above, the straight line will not predict prediction error. This error can be expressed using the following formula:

$$\text{Prediction error} = \text{observed} - \text{predicted} = Y_i - \widehat{Y}_i \tag{7}$$

The sum of the prediction errors for all the observations will produce a total prediction error (TPE). The TPE equation can be seen below:

$$\text{Total prediction error} = \sum (Y_i - \widehat{Y}_i) \tag{8}$$

However, the TPE is ineffective when dealing with positive and negative errors as the positive errors tend to cancel the negative errors. This problem can be overcome by the sum of the squares of the errors (SSE) using the formula below:

$$SSE = \sum (Y_i - \widehat{Y}_i)^2 \tag{9}$$

Using calculus, *a* and *b* can be calculated in a way that the sum of squares presented in the equation above is at a minimum, or 'least' (Lewis-Beck, 1993). As a result, *a* and *b* can be obtained using the following formulas:

$$b = \frac{\sum (X_i - \overline{X})(Y_i - \overline{Y})}{\sum (X_i - \overline{X})^2} \tag{10}$$

$$a = \overline{Y} - b\overline{X} \tag{11}$$

The slope estimate, *b*, shows the average change in the dependent variable associated with a unit change in the independent variable (Y and X respectively in the formula above). However, as mentioned before, the relationships between variables in social sciences are inexact and, therefore, this average change cannot be confirmed in all the cases. In other words, the slope estimate's indication that a unit change in X will cause a certain (average) change in Y may be inappropriate. As a result, the regression of two variables in the real world might only support the idea of causality, not determine it.

The intercept estimate, *a*, indicates the point where the regression line crosses the Y-axis. In other words, it represents the average value of the dependent variable when the independent variable is zero. There are two points to consider when analysing the intercept; first, extrapolation of results to levels beyond the range of data needs to be treated with caution as the researcher would be trying to make generalizations outside the limits of the experiment. Secondly, intercept estimates with a negative value need to be analysed in the particular context of the study as, in many cases, it is impossible to have a value below zero in the real world.

A1.7.1.1 The coefficient of determination R^2

'The coefficient of determination, R^2, indicates the explanatory power of the bivariate regression model. It records the proportion of variation in the independent variable 'explained' or 'accounted for' by the independent variable' (Lewis-Beck, 1993). This coefficient can be calculated using the following equation:

$$R^2 = \frac{\sum (\widehat{Y}_i - \overline{Y})^2}{\sum (Y_i - \overline{Y})^2} \qquad (12)$$

where $\sum (\widehat{Y}_i - \overline{Y})^2$ represents the regression sum of squared deviations (RSS) and $\sum (Y_i - \overline{Y})^2$ the total sum of squared deviations (TSS).

This relationship can be explained by starting the analysis using

$$Y_i = a + b\,Xi + ei \qquad (6)$$

where for each particular value of X_i the formula will calculate a predicted value for $\widehat{Y}_i$. This calculation will account for the difference between the predicted value of the dependent variable and the mean, $\widehat{Y}_i - \overline{Y}$. However, the deviation between the actual value and the predicted value, $Y_i - \widehat{Y}_i$, is still unexplained. In short, there are two deviations that need to be accounted for. If these deviations are squared and then summed, it will be possible to obtain the complete set of variations for the dependent variable. These components can be seen below:

$$\text{RSS} = \sum(\widehat{Y}_i - \overline{Y})^2 \quad \text{and} \quad \text{ESS} = \sum(Y_i - \widehat{Y}_i)^2 \tag{13}$$

where RSS means Regression (explained) Sum of Squared Deviations and ESS Error (unexplained) Sum of Squared Deviations. The Total Sum of Squared Deviations (TSS) equals:

$$\text{TSS} = \text{RSS} + \text{ESS} \tag{14}$$

As mentioned before, TSS indicates the total variation in Y (the independent variable) that the researcher would like to explain, where RSS is accounted for by $Y_i = a + b X_i + e_i$ (the regression equation), but ESS is not accounted for by this regression equation. As a result, 'the larger RSS relative to TSS, the better' (Lewis-Beck, 1993), a concept that sets the basis for the R^2 measure:

$$R^2 = \frac{\text{RSS}}{\text{TSS}} = \frac{\sum(\widehat{Y}_i - \overline{Y})^2}{\sum(Y_i - \overline{Y})^2} \tag{15}$$

This relation can be seen more clearly in Figure A1.4.

The values of R^2 range from 0 to 1, where a value equal to 1 means that the independent variable fully explains the variation in the independent variable, and $R^2 = 0$ means that the independent variable does not explain the variations in the independent variable. Therefore, the closer that R^2 gets to 1, the better the fit of the regression line to the observed points, and the higher the variation in Y explained by X. In other words, a high R^2 (namely over 0.9) is important for the accuracy of the predictions. However, such a high $R^2$is difficult to find in practice (especially in social sciences); as a result, social researchers use this indicator mainly to provide a statistical explanation of phenomena rather than explaining causal relations.

A1.7.1.2 Assumptions behind regression analysis

- *Absence of specification error*: the theoretical model represented in the equation is correct. In other words, the relationship between variables is linear, no relevant independent variable has been deliberately excluded, and no irrelevant independent variable has been improperly included.

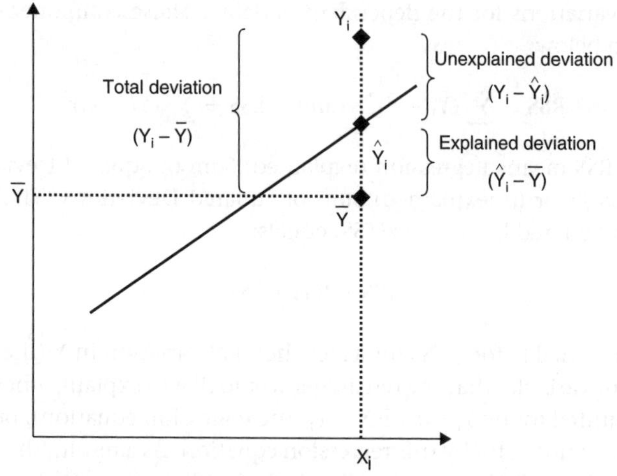

Figure A1.4 Explained and unexplained deviations
Source: Adapted from Lewis-Beck (1993).

- *No measurement error*: the measures are correct and accurate.
- *Zero mean*: the expected value of the error term, e_i, is zero for each observation.
- *Homoskedasticity*: 'the variability in the error term does not depend on any factor included in the analysis' (Schroeder et al., 1986). When this condition is not met, heteroskedasticity exists; a problem most frequently found in cross-sectional studies that could be overcome using a weighted least squares procedure.
- *No autocorrelation or no serial correlation*: the residual errors from different observations are not correlated with the errors of the other observations. In other words, the error of an observation at a certain time is not related to errors of observations at a later time and, therefore, the factors affecting Y in period i are independent from those affecting Y in other periods. Autocorrelation, a problem most frequently found in time-series studies, makes the significance tests and confidence intervals invalid.
- *No multicollinearity*: two or more independent variables used in a regression analysis are independent and, therefore, not correlated. Multicollinearity is likely to be present in most regression analysis as independent variables are unlikely to be totally uncorrelated

(especially in social sciences); as a consequence, the question is about the degree of collinearity and it should be addressed when designing the variables and sources of data.

- 'Error term normally distributed' (Lewis-Beck, 1993): the skewness statistic can show the normality of the frequency distribution, when skewness = 0 the distribution is normal and can be calculated using the formula below:

$$\text{Skewness} = \frac{\sum (y_i - \overline{y})^3}{n} \tag{16}$$

The best linear unbiased estimates will be calculated if the first six assumptions are met. It means that, on average, the unbiased estimators precisely estimate the population parameter, $E(a) = \alpha$ and $E(b) = \beta$. In addition, if the final assumption is also met, the model will calculate the best unbiased estimates, a and b. These estimates can be used in significance tests to establish the probability that the population parameters are different from zero.

There are some discrepancies in the literature on how these assumptions affect the robustness of the regression analysis. On the one hand, some authors argue that regression analysis is robust enough as the parameter estimates will not be greatly affected by violations in the assumptions. On the other hand, others say that if the assumptions are not met the regression analysis could be useless. The point seems to be that some assumptions are more important than others; for example, normality in the error distribution tends to be less important when analysing a large sample as the central-limit theorem can be used (this theorem states that 'the distribution of a sum of independent variables, which we can conceive of the error term as representing, approaches normality as sample size increases, irrespective of the nature of the distributions in the population'; Lewis-Beck, 1993). On the contrary, the exclusion of a relevant independent variable (specification error) can damage the estimation power of the model.

A1.7.1.3 Confidence intervals

Confidence intervals are used to 'carry out tests of whether particular variables make a difference. That is, [social researchers] assume that the true regression coefficient (or set of coefficients) is zero and then assess how likely it is that the estimated coefficients could have occurred by chance. This probability is said to be the significance probability' (Achen, 1982). This assessment can become operational by using a set of two hypotheses generally called the 'null hypothesis' and the 'alternative hypothesis'. The null hypothesis states that X does not have any association with Y and, as a result, the slope β is zero in the population. On the other hand, the alternative hypothesis says that X is associated with Y and, as a consequence, the slope β is not zero in the population. These hypotheses can be seen below:

$$H_0\colon \beta = 0 \text{ (null hypothesis)}$$
$$H_1\colon \beta \neq 0 \text{ (alternative hypothesis)} \tag{17}$$

These hypotheses are tested against an interval built around the slope estimate *b*. The interval could be one-tailed or two-tailed; a two-tailed test means that the effect of X on Y is non-directional and could be upheld if the slope *b* is either negative or positive. The level of confidence depends on the needs of the study, generally over 95% (0.975 for the two-tailed example in the following equation). The confidence interval can be expressed by the following equation:

$$(b \pm t_{n-k-1;0.975} s_b) \tag{18}$$

The t comes from the use of the t distribution. On the other hand, s_b represents an estimate of the standard deviation of *b* (the slope estimate), is usually called the standard error, and can be calculated using the following equation:

$$s_b = \sqrt{\frac{\sum (Y - \hat{Y})^2/(n-2)}{\sum (X - \bar{X})^2}} \tag{19}$$

The t distribution with n – k – 1 ('where n is the number of observations and k the number of independent variables not counting the intercept' (Achen, 1982)) degrees of freedom is used because it would not be technically correct to use the normal distribution to build a confidence interval for β with s_b as an estimate. A confidence interval for the intercept α can also be constructed; in this case, it will attempt to accept (reject) 'the possibility that the regression line cuts the origin' (Lewis-Beck, 1993).

The power of confidence intervals resides in the fact that it allows presenting the results of the parameter estimates as a range rather than as the specific value resulting from the bivariate regression. In other words, bivariate regressions show a point estimate, when confidence intervals present an interval estimate. This distinction is useful in the analysis of the results as the researcher could state that the change in the dependent variable (Y) associated with a unit change in the independent variable (X) falls within a certain range with, for example, 95% certainty.

A1.7.1.4 Significance testing

The equation shown above for a two-tailed, 95% confidence interval for β is used as a starting point to calculate the significance of a test (Lewis-Beck, 1993):

$$(b \pm t_{n-k-1;0.975} s_b) \tag{18}$$

If the confidence interval does not contain zero, the equation can be re-written:

$$\begin{aligned} &(b - t_{n-k-1;0.975} s_b) > 0 \quad \text{when b is positive,} \\ \text{or} \quad &(b + t_{n-k-1;0.975} s_b) < 0 \quad \text{when b is negative} \end{aligned} \tag{20}$$

and using calculus can be restated as:

$$\begin{aligned} &(b/s_b > t_{n-k-1;0.975}) \quad \text{when b is positive,} \\ \text{or} \quad &(b/s_b < t_{n-k-1;0.975}) \quad \text{when b is negative} \end{aligned} \tag{21}$$

These two formulas can be merged and written as:

$$|b/s_b| > t_{n-k-1;0.975} \tag{22}$$

which can be read as when the absolute value of b, the parameter estimate, divided by s_b, its standard error, is higher than $t_{n-k-1;0.975}$, the t distribution value; H_0: $\beta = 0$, the null hypothesis, is rejected. In other words, it can be said that the parameter estimates, *a* and *b*, are statistically significant at the 0.5 level (in the two-tailed example above) if the inequality shown in this equation is verified. The division b/s_b is also known as the t ratio.

Lewis-Beck (1993) states that among the reasons why a parameter estimate may not be significant are:

- 'Inadequate sample size,
- 'Type II error [accepting the null hypothesis when it is false],
- Specification error, and
- Restricted variance in X'.

A1.7.1.5 Multiple regression

Multiple regression includes more than one independent variable in the regression equation and could be used as 'a method for measuring the effects of several factors concurrently' (Schroeder et al., 1986). By doing this, the regression equation can give more powerful explanations as most events tend to depend on more than one cause. The multiple regression equation can be seen below

$$Y = a_0 + b_1 X_1 + b_2 X_2 + b_3 X_3 + \cdots + b_n X_n + e \tag{23}$$

where the subscripts identify the different independent variables, X. In multiple regression, the assumptions, interpretations, the R^2 (coefficient of determination), the confidence intervals, and the significance test are applied in the same way as in bivariate regression. In addition, the least squares principle, $SSE = \sum (Y_i - Y_i)^2$ (Equation 9), is also applied to estimate the parameters.

The intercepts in multiple regression are interpreted in the following way: a_0, the intercept estimate, represents the value of Y when the value of each independent variable equals zero. On the other hand, b_n, the slope estimate, shows the average change in the independent variable Y as a result of a unit change in one of the independent variables, X_n, when the other independent variables remain constant. For this reason, this slope is called 'partial slope or partial regression coefficient' (Lewis-Beck, 1993).

In multiple regression, the problem of multicollinearity described above (section 0 Assumptions) becomes more relevant as more variables are included in the model. In this context, the bigger problem seems to be perfect multicollinearity, when one of the independent variables is perfectly correlated with another independent variable. This perfect multicollinearity is relatively easy to spot as it will not be possible to find one unique solution for the least square parameters estimates; however, high (instead of perfect) multicollinearity seems to be more difficult to spot. As mentioned above, in social sciences it is highly probable that variables are correlated; therefore, the question should be about the degree of this correlation. One of the usual symptoms of high multicollinearity is a significant R^2 for the equation, but with coefficients that show statistical insignificance. Another symptom is a regression coefficient with big changes when an independent variable is included or excluded in the model. A third symptom could be a surprisingly large or small coefficient that could be rejected because it does not make any sense in the context of the study. Finally, the sign of the coefficient could be seen as a symptom of multicollinearity; however, in a non-experimental study it will be difficult to know the sign beforehand.

Although the symptoms described above are a good starting point, they do not prove whether the problem exists or not. The researcher should analyse the intercorrelation of the independent variables looking for high coefficients (0.8 or above), and then study the relationship between one independent variable with all the other independent variables; in other words, regressing each independent variable on all the other independent variables. The analysis of the R^2, the coefficient of determination, will show the degree of such a relationship.

A1.7.1.6 Stepwise multiple regression

Stepwise multiple regression aims to 'determine which variables explain the greatest and significant proportions of the variance in the variable of interest and what these proportions are' (Cramer, 2004). This is achieved by entering first the independent variable with the highest statistically significant correlation with the independent variable into the regression analysis. This method is useful when analysing many independent variables and when the relative importance of these variables is not known beforehand. In this context, stepwise multiple regression shows the variable that was entered first in the regression along with how much of the variance in the dependent variable is explained by this independent variable. The process is repeated many times as independent variables are present in the model, showing the independent variable that was entered second, third, fourth, etc., and how much of the variance in the dependent variable they explain. As a result, the importance of each independent variable ranked by its explanation of the variance in the dependent variable is obtained.

A1.7.1.7 Regression with dummy variables

Regression analysis is a flexible and useful method for quantitative analysis, but its usefulness would be restricted if the independent variables had to be measured on interval scales. This is especially true for social sciences, where many variables are of a qualitative nature. Therefore, when independent variables are qualitative, a technique is needed to present these variables in a quantitative way which represents the richness of the qualitative information. In this context, the use of dummy variables allows the researcher 'to capture the information contained in a categorization scheme and then to use this information in a standard regression estimation' (Hardy, 1993). In other words, dummy variables present a useful technique to use qualitative information in quantitative analysis.

As mentioned above, dummy variables are constructed trying to contain all the information in the original qualitative scale; where a variable with k categories will require k – 1 dummy variables to get this information. The reason behind the use of k – 1 dummy variables can be found in the assumption of no perfect multicollinearity among independent variables, which 'requires that none of the explanatory variables can be written as a perfect linear combination of remaining explanatory variables in the model' (Hardy, 1993). For example, when the original variable has only two categories, *Yes* and *No*, only one dummy variable is enough to get all the information using the following structure *Yes* = 1 – *No*, leaving the data contained in *No* as redundant and not necessary for the calculations. The category not used as a dummy variable, *No* in the example, is used as what is called the 'reference group'. By using this structure, each dummy variable records the presence or absence of a category in the original variable; therefore, the information is not altered, only shown in a different way. As a result, the interpretation of the regression coefficients should be adjusted 'to be consistent with the underlying measurement properties of the independent variables' (Hardy, 1993).

A1.7.2 Qualitative data analysis

Qualitative analysis can offer research works a different perspective by including the richness of the data collected. This, for example, can be seen in the amount of information present in an interview that is not usually considered in the variables and/or interrelations generally used in quantitative analyses, such as the voice tones, the tension, the hierarchy, the body language, etc. In this context, Gummesson (2006) claimed that the value of qualitative analysis (in comparison with that of quantitative methods) can be found in three areas. The first area is complexity; quantitative methods mainly attempt to reduce complexity by selecting only a few variables when reality is complex by nature; on the contrary, qualitative analysis offers condensation, making each concept, model, and theory progressively denser with knowledge' and uses 'variables and concepts that absorb the core of a phenomenon without disfiguring its nature'. The second area is context, as society and business are a network of relationships it is difficult to isolate the study of events from their context; in this sense, qualitative analysis tends to offer 'more realism and relevance'. The third area is persona, as sometimes it is difficult to disconnect the person from the investigations, the researcher has 'a decisive say in both the design and outcome of a study' specially in the field of management where 'data and their relationships are incomplete' (Gummesson, 2006).

'The basis of all qualitative analysis is effective coding of collected data' (Pole & Lampard, 2002). By coding, researchers attempt to gather the most important facts or ideas from the data in a short and clear form 'through the identification of a series of descriptors which act as signposts to the collected data' (Pole & Lampard, 2002). This first process is usually called 'open coding' and allows researchers to review the data in a way that allows the richness and detail to be more easily identified. As a consequence, coding could be seen as a reductionist process, but at the same time, it offers the possibility of being expansive. The literature is not uniform in the definition of coding mainly 'because there is no guarantee that researchers always take the same approach to coding' (Pole & Lampard, 2002). In this sense, Bryman and Burgess (1994) said that 'there is the potential for considerable confusion regarding what coding actually is, so that it is doubtful whether writers who employ the term are referring to the same procedure'.

The process of coding is mostly based on the 'Grounded Theory' developed by Glaser and Strauss (1967). This was one of the first systematic approaches to developing theory from qualitative research and has become the benchmark for qualitative analysis. The identification of codes gives research works a sense that goes beyond the detail of the data as it offers a more abstract and conceptual perspective. This is mainly because the identification of these codes is an important part of theory discovery; they allow researchers to build general ideas of the matter under study. Miles and Huberman (1984) said that codes could be descriptive, interpretative, and explanatory; however it is recognised that the boundaries of each classification are not clear as 'codes are based on interpretation or analysis by the researcher. They are not objective, uncontested artefacts. Rather, they are the result of the researcher's interaction with the data' (Pole & Lampard, 2002).

For the analysis of qualitative data, Glaser and Strauss (1967) proposed four general approaches. In the first approach (1), the researcher codes the data at the beginning and then analyses it; in other words, s/he transforms qualitative data into quantifiable form. The second approach (2) is mainly for generating new theoretical ideas, categories, hypotheses, and their interrelation, where the researcher redesigns and reintegrates the theoretical conception as the data is being reviewed. The third approach (3) combines the previous two: the analytic procedure of (1) and the theory development of (2), with the purpose of generating theory in a more systematic fashion. The final and fourth approach (4) is called analytic induction, which also combines (1) and (2) and has 'been concerned with generating and proving an integrated, limited, precise, universally applicable theory of causes accounting for a specific behaviour' (Glaser & Strauss, 1967). The use of these approaches in relation to the purposes of the research can be seen in Table A1.3.

Glaser and Strauss (1967) also proposed four steps for the analysis of qualitative data. The first step involves the comparison of incidents applicable to each category, which means coding the data into 'as many categories of analysis as possible, as categories emerge, or as data emerge that fit an existing theory'. As coding goes on, the researcher should compare the codes with those of 'previous incidents in the same and different groups coded in the same category' and, as a consequence, this constant comparison soon begins to 'generate theoretical properties of the category'. The second step integrates

Table A1.3 Use of approaches to qualitative research

Generating theory	Provisional testing of theory	
	Yes	No
Yes	Combining inspection for hypothesis (2) along with coding for test, then analysing data (1) analytic deduction (4)	Inspection for hypotheses (2) Constant comparative methods (3)
No	Coding for test, then analysing data (1)	Ethnographic description

Source: Glaser & Strauss (1967).

the categories and their properties; this happens as a consequence of the constant process of comparison, at the beginning is a comparison of incidents and, as the process continues, the comparison is between an incident and the 'properties of the category that resulted from initial comparison of incidents'. 'Constant comparison causes the accumulated knowledge pertaining to a property of the category to readily start to become integrated; that is, related in many different ways, resulting in a unified whole'. 'Thus the theory develops, as different categories and their properties tend to become integrated through constant comparisons that force the analyst to make some related theoretical sense of each comparison' (Glaser & Strauss, 1967).

The third step means the delimitation of the theory, which occurs as theory develops and the constant comparison process begins to bring less new findings. The delimitation takes place at two levels: (i) the theory 'in the sense that major modifications become fewer and fewer as the analyst compares the next incidents of a category to its properties'; and (ii) the categories which suffer a 'reduction in the original list for coding' as theory grows, and is also delimited because the list of categories 'become theoretically saturated'. The fourth and final step is the writing of theory, where 'the constant comparative method makes probable the achievement of a complex theory that corresponds closely to the data, since the constant comparisons force the analyst to consider much diversity in the data. By diversity we [the authors] mean that each incident is compared with other incidents, or with properties of a category, in terms as many similarities and differences as possible' (Glaser & Strauss, 1967).

Although the process described above has provided a sound methodological framework for the analysis of qualitative data, many voices criticize qualitative analyses as they sometimes appear to be 'little more than a reflection of the creative ability of the researcher, who tells a story based on the data in a similar way to a novelist' (Pole & Lampard, 2002). The question here is about the reliability and validity (see section A1.4 for their definitions) of qualitative analyses. The main problem seems to be that these concepts are usually associated with quantitative studies as for this type of research it is relatively easy to determine the reliability of the results in statistical terms, and to replicate the study at a later date. In an attempt to overcome these problems of reliability, Dey (1993) proposed to 'open up a study to public scrutiny,... which includes allowing other researchers and interested parties to assess not only the findings of a qualitative research but also the means by which they were reached' (Pole & Lampard, 2002) as repetition of qualitative works is possible only on rare occasions. Regarding the validity of a research work, Dey (1993) said that it depends to a certain extent on how 'well grounded conceptually and empirically' is an account, which could be interpreted as 'the extent to which an account is embedded within the data, and to the capacity of the researcher to support his/her findings with relevant, detailed examples from those data' (Pole & Lampard, 2002).

A1.7.3 Quantitative and qualitative analyses

As mentioned at the end of the previous chapter, this work considers both quantitative and qualitative analyses. These two types of analyses were explained in sections A1.7.1 and A1.7.2 above. The use of a mixed method is based on the objectives of this work (stated in section 4.4) of offering a broader approach to the analysis.

Four factors need to be considered when using mixed methods: (i) implementation, to signal if the data (quantitative or qualitative) is collected in phases (sequentially) or at the same time (concurrently); (ii) priority, which means the weight given to the quantitative or the qualitative approaches; (iii) integration considers at which stage of the process the combination of the two types of data will occur; and (iv) theoretical perspective, which may be one from the social sciences

Table A1.4 Decision choices for determining a mixed methods strategy of enquiry

Implementation	Priority	Integration	Theoretical perspective
No sequence – concurrent	Equal	At data collection	Explicit
Sequential-qualitative first	Qualitative	At data analysis	Implicit
Sequential-quantitative first	Quantitative	At data interpretation	
		With some combination	

Source: Creswell et al. (2003).

or from an advocacy/participatory lens (Creswell, 2003). Table A1.4 shows the choices for determining a mixed methods strategy.

Creswell et al. (2003) proposed six different strategies resulting from the combination of the four areas shown in the previous figure. In the first strategy, sequential explanatory, the quantitative data are usually collected before the qualitative data (priority is given to the former), the two methods are combined during the interpretation of the findings, and the study may or may not have a specific theoretical framework. It is mainly used when qualitative analysis is needed to assist in the explanation and interpretation of the quantitative study. The second strategy is the sequential exploratory; it is similar to the previous one, but with the qualitative analysis taking the lead; qualitative data are collected first and receives priority over quantitative, which are used to support the findings from the qualitative study. The third strategy is called sequential transformative; it also has two collection stages but either method could be used first, and priority can be given to the quantitative or the qualitative analyses. This strategy is generally used within a theoretical perspective to guide the study, and its purpose is to allow the researcher to apply the method that serves her/his theoretical perspective best.

Fourth comes the concurrent triangulation strategy which is 'selected as the model when a researcher uses two different methods in an attempt to confirm, cross-validate, or corroborate findings within a single study' (Creswell, 2003). The use of qualitative and quantitative analysis is aimed at offsetting the weaknesses of the other method, the data collection is usually concurrent, priority is given to either the quantitative or qualitative analysis, and the integration occurs during the interpretation phase. This interpretation is used to strengthen the confluence (if any) of the findings, or to understand the differences. The fifth strategy is denominated concurrent nested, where the data are collected simultaneously, one approach has priority over the other so the one with the lowest priority is 'nested' within the dominant method, the data are mixed during the analysis stage, and may or may not have a certain theoretical perspective. Finally, the sixth is the concurrent transformative strategy which 'is guided by the researcher's use of a specific theoretical perspective' (Creswell, 2003). In these six strategies, the validity and the reliability of mixed methods is assessed during the quantitative and qualitative analysis phases (Tashakkori & Teddlie, 1998).

A1.8 Conclusion

This appendix has attempted to give an overview of the theoretical framework of the methodology employed in this research work. Chapter 5 shows how these concepts were applied to the specific situations under study as well as further analyses when needed.

Appendix 2: European Companies in South America That Could Be Included in the Population

ABB Asea Brown Boveri	Electrolux Group	Lufthansa Group
ABN AMRO	Eletricidade de Portugal	LVMH
Adecco	Endesa	Man Ferrostaal
Akzo Nobel	Enel	Mannesmann
Alcatel	ENI	Marconi
Allianz	E-on	Metro
Alstom	Ericsson	Michelin
Anglo American	Experian	Movistar
Assicurazioni Generali	Fiat	Nestlé
AstraZeneca	France Telecom	NH Hoteles
Atofina	Gas Natural	Nokia
Aventis S.A.	GEA Group	Norsk Hydro
Banco Bilbao Vizcaya Argentaria	Glaxo Wellcome	Novartis
Banque Nationale de Paris	Groupe Casino	O. Fournier
BASF	Groupe Danone	Olivetti
Bayer	Grupo Marsans	Pirelli
Bertelsmann	Grupo RTR	Portugal Telecom
BMW	Halcrow	P&O
BP	Henkel	Porsche
British American Tobacco	Hoechst	PSA Peugeot-Citroen
BT	HSBC Holdings	Puratos
Carrefour	HypoVereinsbank	Rabobank
Chateau Montviel	Iberdrola	Reed Elsevier
CNP Assurances	Imperial Chemical Industries	Renault
Commerzbank	ING Group	Repsol YPF
Crédit Agricole	Invensys	Rhône-Poulenc
Crédit Lyonnais	Ipsos	Robert Bosch
Daimler Chrysler	L'Oréal	Roche
Degussa	Lafarge	Royal & Sun Alliance
Deutsche Bank	Lagardère Groupe	Royal Dutch/Shell Group
Diageo plc	Lanxess	Royal Philips Electronics
Dresdner Bank	Lloyds TSB Group	Saint-Gobain
EDF		Santander Group
		Saur

(*Continued*)

(Continued)

Scania	Swarovski	Unilever
SEPI	Telecom Italia	UPM-Kymmene
Siemens	Telefónica	Vivendi Universal
Société Générale	ThyssenKrupp	Volkswagen
Sodexho Pass	Total Fina Elf	Volvo
Sonae Distribuição	UBS	Wartsila
Statoil	UniCredit	Zurich
Suez Lyonnaise des Eaux		

Appendix 3: Responses to the Structured Questions (Selected Answers)

In terms of ownership structure of foreign investments, which of the following describes your company's policy?

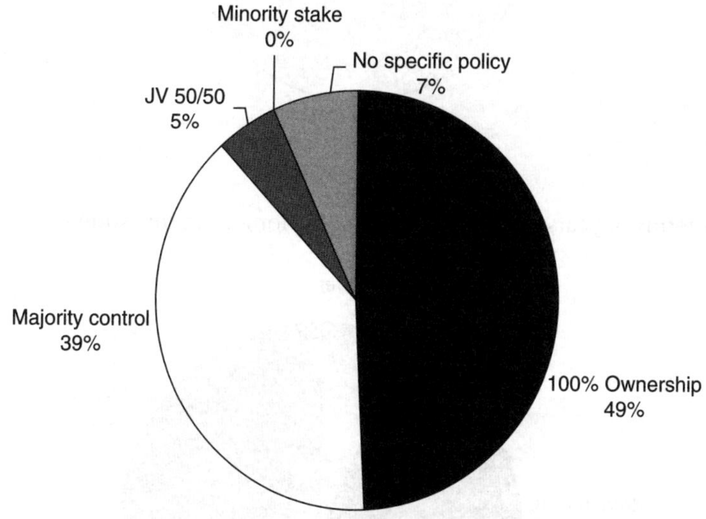

Without taking into consideration any other criteria, where is your company more likely to make the next long-term investment?

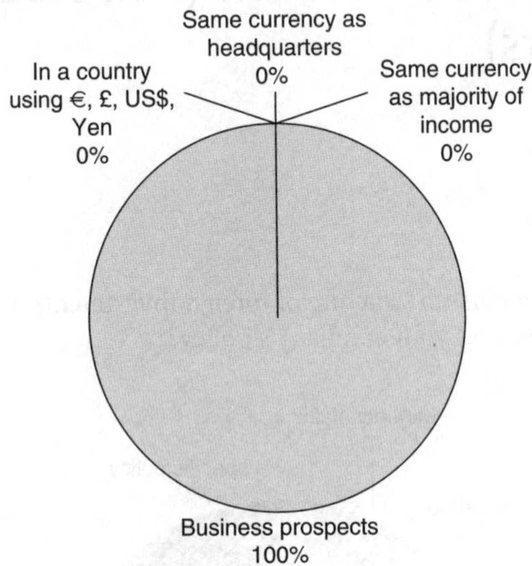

In terms of years, what do you mean by 'long-term investments'?

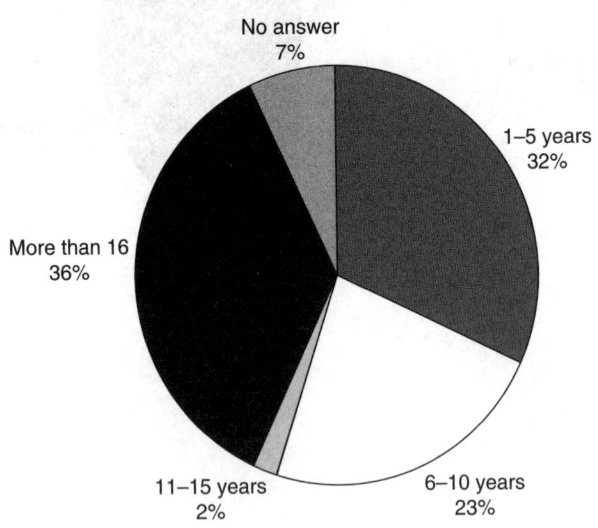

Does your company take into consideration this economic exposure when investing abroad? In which stage?

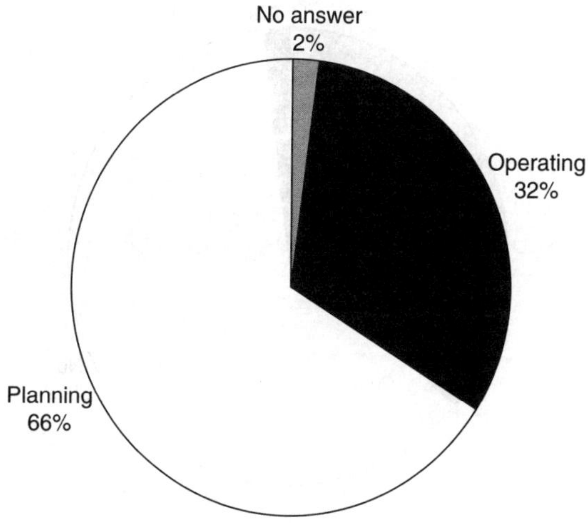

Once the subsidiaries are operating abroad, does your company study what the competitors do to protect their investments against economic exposure?

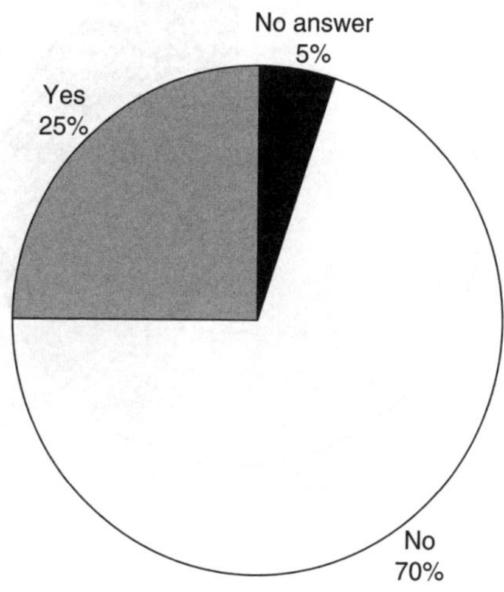

Has your company developed an exchange rate hedging policy?

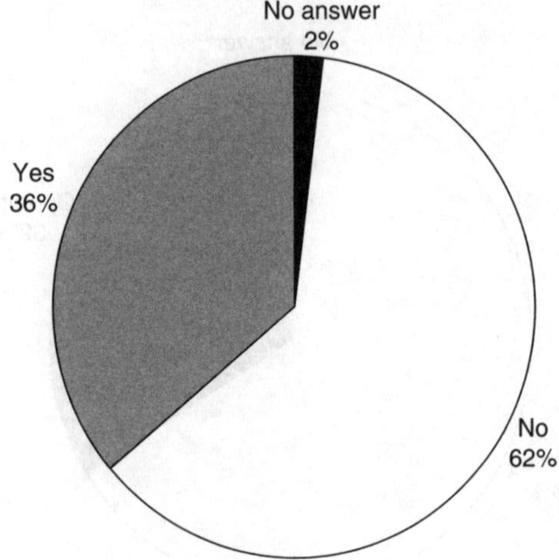

When your company assesses the exchange rate risk, does it include other departments besides finance?

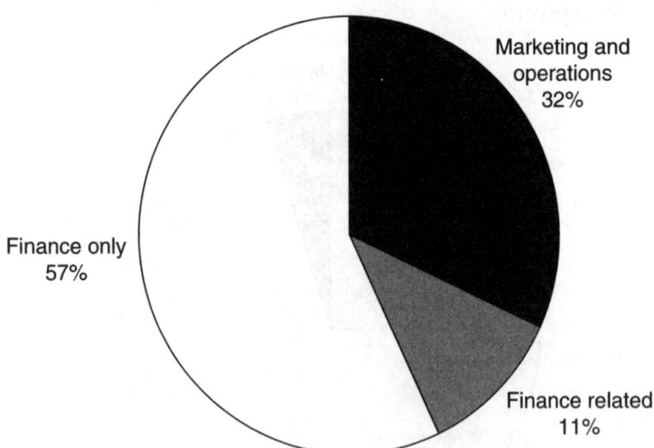

What degrees of freedom do the subsidiaries have in hedging their exchange rate exposure in terms of decision-making?

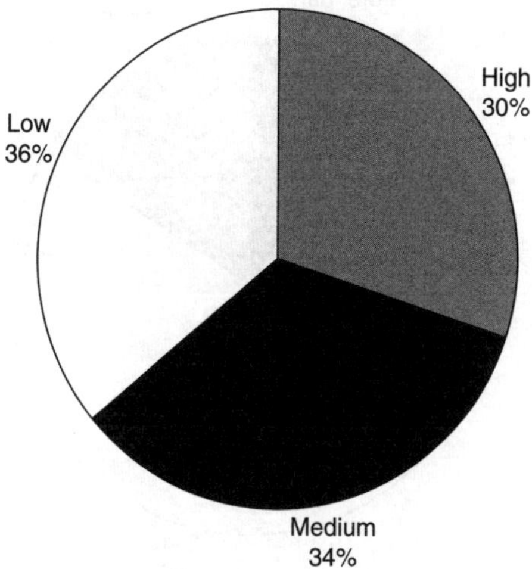

What degrees of freedom do the subsidiaries have in hedging their exchange rate exposure in terms of implementation?

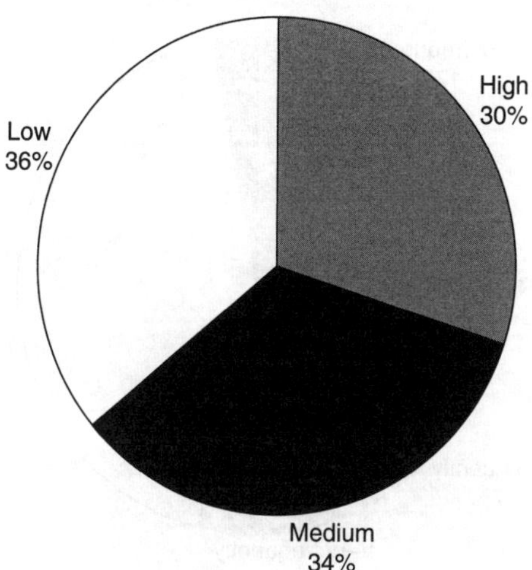

In terms of percentage, from what variation level will you start considering exchange rate as a risk?

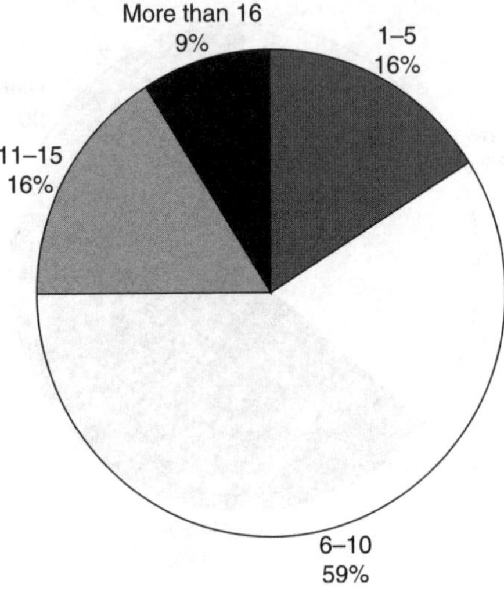

Please could you tell me the relative use of the following hedging techniques in emerging markets?

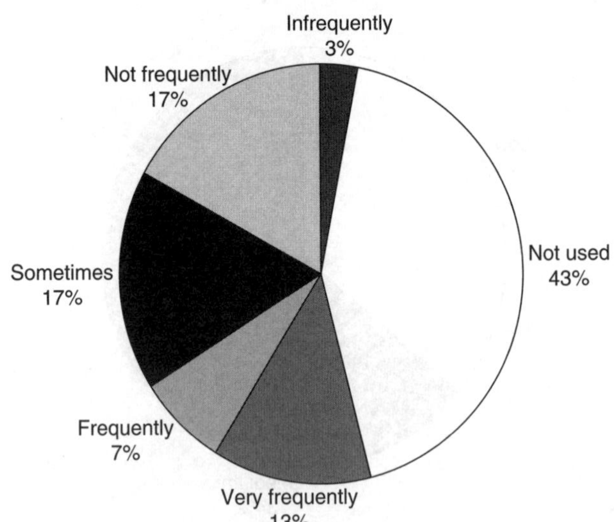

Appendix 4: Correlation Matrix

	INDUSTRY	CURRENCIES	ORIGIN	COUNTRIES	OWNERSHIP	NEXTINVEST	IHORIZON	STAGE2	BENCHMARK2	FXPOLICY2	AREAS2	AREAS3	AUTDECISION2	AUTDECISION3	AUTIMPLEMENT2	AUTIMPLEMENT3	ERRISK	HTUSE
INDUSTRY	1.00																	
CURRENCIES	−0.11	1.00																
ORIGIN	−0.33	0.08	1.00															
COUNTRIES	−0.07	.410*	−0.13	1.00														
OWNERSHIP	−0.22	−0.17	0.17	−0.08	1.00													
NEXTINVEST	.(a)	.(a)	.(a)	.(a)	.(a)	.(a)												
IHORIZON	−.5**	0.26	0.24	0.08	0.25	.(a)	1.00											
STAGE2	−0.36	0.10	0.29	−0.13	−0.05	.(a)	0.23	1.00										
BENCHMARK2	0.14	0.05	0.25	0.12	0.00	.(a)	0.00	−0.22	1.00									
FXPOLICY2	−0.04	0.34	0.34	0.14	−0.22	.(a)	0.20	.471*	0.02	1.00								
AREAS2	−0.09	0.14	0.19	0.06	−0.20	.(a)	0.31	0.19	0.36	0.30	1.00							
AREAS3	−.41*	−0.36	0.12	−0.15	0.16	.(a)	0.32	0.04	−.42*	−0.08	−.39*	1.00						
AUTDECISION2	−0.06	0.39	.400*	0.16	−0.12	.(a)	−0.04	0.36	−0.03	.5**	0.37	−.42*	1.00					
AUTDECISION3	−0.08	−0.22	−0.21	−0.25	0.23	.(a)	0.06	0.01	−0.08	−0.39	−0.23	0.24	−.6**	1.00				
AUTIMPLEMENT2	−0.10	0.39	.400*	0.16	−0.21	.(a)	−0.04	0.36	−0.03	.5**	0.37	−.42*	.8**	−.6**	1.00			
AUTIMPLEMENT3	−0.08	−0.22	−0.21	−0.25	0.23	.(a)	0.06	0.01	−0.08	−0.39	−0.23	0.24	−.6**	1.**	−.6**	1.00		
ERRISK	−.51*	−0.07	0.44	−0.29	0.26	.(a)	0.44	.6**	−0.09	0.37	.(a)	0.09	0.24	0.02	0.07	0.02	1.00	
HTUSE	−0.31	.558*	0.27	0.22	0.20	.(a)	0.32	0.17	−0.15	0.42	(a)	−0.06	.538*	−0.32	0.39	−0.32	0.06	1.00

* Correlation is significant at the 0.05 level (2–tailed).
** Correlation is significant at the 0.01 level (2–tailed).
[a] Cannot be computed because at least one of the variables is constant.

Notes

1 Introduction

1. Quoted in S. Brittan, 'The Dollar Needs Benign Neglect', *Financial Times*, 30 January 2004.
2. See, for example, Lawrence Lau and Joseph Stiglitz, 'China's Alternative to Revaluation', *Financial Times*, 24 April 2005.

2 The Global Economy and the Emerging Markets

1. Note: in this table, developed countries include Canada, the United States, EU, EFTA, Japan, Australia, and New Zealand; transition countries include the former Soviet Union, Eastern and Central Europe, the Baltic States, and the Balkans; the remaining countries are classified as developing.
2. Note: estimates are calculated on the basis of the 113 agreements covering trade in goods notified to the WTO and in force as of July 2000, using trade data for 1999.
3. The terms 'less developed country', 'emerging economy' and 'emerging market' will be used interchangeably in the following sections.

3 Review of the Literature

1. It is not the intention of this work discussing different methods of discounting future cash flows.

5 How the Analysis Was Carried Out

1. The dummy variable trap could happen when all the dummy variables are included in a model producing a linear relationship between the dummy variables and the intercept.
2. This is not an attempt to develop Grounded Theory, only its systematic approach was applied to analyse the qualitative data.
3. A method suggested by Glaser and Strauss to collect data in which 'beyond the initial collection of data, further collection cannot be planned in advance of the emerging theory. The emerging theory points to the next steps... The criteria for choosing samples are those of theoretical purpose and relevance... The researcher chooses any groups that will help generate, to the fullest extent, as many properties of the categories as possible'. The process continues until the point of theoretical saturation, when 'there is no additional data that can be found whereby the sociologist can develop properties of category' (Glaser and Strauss, 1967, pp. 47–64).

6 The Analysis of the Data

1. Austria, ATX; Italy, Mibtel; Sweden, OMX30; Finland, OMX25; Germany, DAX; France, CAC40; UK, FTSE100; Spain, IBEX35; Netherlands, AEX; Belgium, BEL20.
2. The weighting was 31.3 per cent Argentina, 58.79 per cent Brazil, and 9.91 per cent Chile, which represents the average weight of the destination of European FDI (ECLAC, 2001).
3. www.bcra.gov.ar, www.ipeadata.gov.br, and www.bcentral.cl for Argentina, Brazil, and Chile respectively retrieved on 25 September 2006. The Multilateral Real Exchange Index calculated by these three governmental agencies was included in the regression. This index considers the inflation of each country and that of its trading partners to calculate the index, and automatically adjusts the weighting of each country according to the variations in the weight of the exports/imports to this country.
4. A period covering the start, development, and aftermath of the latest currency crises in Latin America. Missing values were replaced with the mean of the nearby points.
5. These calculations did not include Co 2, Co 10, Co 23, Co 26, Co 30, and Co 33 as they were considered outliers and therefore may affect the linear relationship; consequently, they were dropped from the analysis. Outliers were defined as < Q1-5(Q3-Q1) or > Q3-5(Q3-Q1).
6. ORIGIN was entered first and explained about 15.5 per cent of the variance in the independent variable; FXPOLICY2 was entered second and explained a further 14.4 per cent; and AUTIMPLEMENT2 was entered third and explained another 11.5 per cent. The three enters are significant at the 0.05 level.
7. See qualitative analysis.
8. See qualitative analysis.
9. The dataset was reproduced twice, keeping the same order and structure.
10. It is important to highlight that the results obtained by regressing the artificially increased sample were used only to test the statistical significance of the findings obtained in previous regressions and not to draw conclusions.
11. $d = 1.542$; $(4 - d) > du;0.01$ $(4 - 1.542 > 1.635)$ shows statistical significance that the error terms are not negatively autocorrelated; $dL;0.01 < d < du;0.01$ $(0.782 < 1.542 < 1.635)$ shows that the test is inconclusive for positive autocorrelation.
12. White proposed to analyse the R^2 of a regression equation that includes the squared residuals from a regression model with the cross-product of the regressors and squared regressors.
13. Interview with a Director of one of the largest Spanish investors, Spain, February 2005.
14. Interview with the CFO for Latin America of a French service company, Argentina, August 2005.
15. Interview with the CEO of a French power generation company, Argentina, July 2005.

16. Interview with the Deputy Director of Finance for Chile of one of the largest Spanish investors, Chile, August 2005. Similar comments were made by other interviewees, and also highlighted in an interview with the Director for the Americas of a large French investor, Argentina, August 2005.
17. Interview with the COO of an Austrian manufacturing company, Argentina, July 2005. Similar comments were made by other participants, and also stressed in an interview with the COO of a British manufacturing company, Argentina, July 2005.
18. Interview with the CEO of a French power generation company, Argentina, July 2005.
19. Interview with the Finance Director of one of the top Spanish investors, Spain, March 2005.
20. Interview with the Director of Risk Analysis of one of the top Spanish investors, Spain, March 2005.
21. Interview with the COO of one of the companies in the sample, Argentina, July 2005.
22. Interview with the President for Latin America of a British company, USA, May 2005.
23. Interview with the Director of Operations of a French manufacturing company, Argentina, July 2005.
24. Interview with a director of a power generation and distribution company, one of the top Spanish investors, Spain, February 2005.
25. Interview with the Corporate Affairs Director of a British manufacturing company, Argentina, August 2005.
26. Interview with the International Director of one of the large Spanish investors, Spain, March 2005.
27. Interview with the Director for the Americas of a large French investor, Argentina, August 2005.
28. Interview with the General Director of a French utility company, Argentina, July 2005.
29. Interview with the CEO of a French power generation company, Argentina, July 2005.
30. Interview with the Planning and Development Director of a British company, Argentina, August 2005.
31. Interview with the COO of a British company, Argentina, July 2005.
32. Interview with a director of one of the largest Spanish investors, Spain, February 2005.
33. Interview with the Director of Operations of a French company, Argentina, July 2005.
34. Interview with the Regional Director for Central and South America of a Belgium manufacturing company, Chile, August 2005.
35. Interview with the CEO of a German company, Argentina, July 2005.
36. Interview with the General Director of a French company, Argentina, July 2005.
37. Interview with the President and Head of Southern Cone and Andes of one of the companies in the sample, Argentina, August 2005.

38. Interview with a Senior Manager of a German company, Argentina, August 2005.
39. Interview with the General Director of a French utility company, Argentina, July 2005.
40. Interview with a Senior Manager of a German company, Argentina, August 2005.
41. Interview with the COO of a British company, Argentina, August 2005.
42. Interview with a Senior Manager of one of the German companies in the sample, Argentina, August 2005.
43. Interview with the President and Head of Southern Cone and Andes of one of the companies in the sample, Argentina, August 2005.
44. Interview with the CEO of a Dutch company, Argentina, July 2005.
45. Interview with the President of a Spanish company, Argentina, July 2005.
46. Interview with the COO of an Austrian company, Argentina, July 2005.
47. Interview with the Director of Operations of a French company, Argentina, July 2005.
48. Interview with the Planning and Development Director of a British company, Argentina, August 2005.
49. Interview with a Senior Manager of a German company, Argentina, August 2005.
50. Interview with a Senior Manager of a Spanish company, Argentina, August 2005.
51. Interview with the Planning and Development Director of a British company, Argentina, August 2005.
52. Interview with a Senior Manager of a German manufacturing company, Argentina, August 2005.
53. Interview with the Director of Operations of a French company, Argentina, July 2005.
54. Interview with the Director of Operations of a French company, Argentina, July 2005.
55. Interview with the COO of a British company, Argentina, July 2005.
56. Interview with a Senior Manager of a British service company, Argentina, August 2005.
57. Interview with the Director of Operations of a French company, Argentina, July 2005.
58. Interview with a Director of a Spanish service company, Argentina, July 2005.
59. Interview with the Regional Director for Central and South America of a Belgian manufacturing company, Chile, August 2005.
60. Interview with the President and Head of Southern Cone and Andes of a Swedish company, Argentina, August 2005.
61. Interview with the General Director of a French company, Argentina, August 2005.
62. Interview with the COO of a British manufacturing company, Argentina, July 2005.
63. Interview with the Chief Economist of one of the largest Spanish investors, Spain, February 2005.

8 An Example of the Use of the Tool

1. Missing values were replaced with the mean of the nearby points.
2. Equity return data and market indexes were sourced from Datastream International, exchange rate information from the countries' central banks and OECD Main Economic Indicators.
3. For multi-country studies this coherence and consistency should be considered.
4. A further study of the companies' earning power (Shapiro, 2003) or using a cash flow-based model (rather the market-based model used in this exercise) would be necessary to make a more conclusive assessment of the effectiveness of their hedging activities.

References

Achen, C. (1982) *Interpreting and Using Regression*. Beverly Hills, CA: Sage.

Aggarwal, R. and L. Soenen (1989) 'Managing Persistent Real Changes in Currency Values: the Role of Multinational Operating Strategies', *Columbia Journal of World Business*, Fall: 60–7.

Alfaro, L. and E. Clavell (2002) 'Foreign Direct Investment', *Harvard Business School Cases*.

Allayannis, G., J. Ihrig and J. Weston (2001) 'Exchange-rate Hedging: Financial Versus Operational Strategies', *American Economic Review*, 91: 391–5.

Allayannis, G. and E. Ofek (2001) 'Exchange Rate Exposure, Hedging, and the Use of Foreign Currency Derivatives', *Journal of International Money and Finance*, 20: 273–96.

Amihud, Y. (1994) 'Exchange Rates and the Valuation of Equity Shares', in Y.A.R. Levich (ed.), *Exchange Rates and Corporate Performance*. Homewood, IL: Irwin.

Arahuetes, A. and R. Casilda (2004) 'Spain', in Z. Vodusek (ed.), *Foreign Direct Investment in Latin America: The Role of European Investors. An Update*. Paris: Inter-American Development Bank.

Arnold, D.J. and J.A. Quelch (1998) 'New Strategies in Emerging Markets', *Sloan Management Review*, 40(1): 7.

Aulakh, P.S., M. Kotabe and H. Teegen (2000) 'Export Strategies and Performance of Firms from Emerging Economies: Evidence from Brazil, Chile and Mexico', *Academy of Management Journal*, 43(3): 342.

Barney, J. (1991) 'Firm Resources and Sustained Competitive Advantage', *Journal of Management* 17: 99–120.

Baron, D.P. (1976) 'Fluctuating Exchange Rates and the Pricing of Exports', *Economic Inquiry*, 14(3): 425.

Bartov, E. and G. Bodnar (1994) 'Firm Valuation, Earnings Expectations and the Exchange-rate Exposure Effect', *Journal of Finance*, 49: 1755–85.

Batten, J., R. Mellor and V. Wan (1993) 'Foreign Exchange Risk Management Practices and Products used by Australian Firms', *Journal of International Business Studies*, Third Quarter: 557–73.

Begg, D., S. Fischer and R. Dornbusch (2000) *Economics*. London: McGraw Hill.

Bodnar, G., A. de Jong and V. Macrae (2003) 'The Impact of Institutional Differences on Derivatives Usage: a Comparative Study of US and Dutch Firms', *European Financial Management*, 9: 271–98.

Bodnar, G. and G. Gebbhardt (1999) 'Derivatives Usage in Risk Management by US and German Non-financial Firms: a Comparative Survey', *Journal of International Financial Management and Accounting*, 10(3): 153–87.

Bodnar, G. and W. Gentry (1993) 'Exchange Rate Exposure and Industry Characteristics: Evidence from Canada, Japan, and the USA', *Journal of International Money and Finance*, 12: 29–45.

Bodnar, G., G. Hayt and R. Marston (1998) '1998 Wharton Survey of Financial Risk Management by US Non-financial Firms', *Financial Management*, 27: 70–91.

Bosworth, B.P. and S.M. Collins (1999) *Capital Flows to Developing Economies: Implications for Saving and Investment*. Washington, DC: Brookings Institution Press.

Brakman, S., H. Garretsen, C. van Marrewijk and A. van Witteloostuijn (2006) *Nations and Firms in the Global Economy: An Introduction to international Economics and Business*. Cambridge: Cambridge University Press.

Breitman, R.L. and J.M. Lucas, J.M. (1987) 'PLANETS: A Modeling System for Business Planning', *Interfaces*, 17(1): 94.

Brewer, T. and S. Young (1998) *The Multilateral Investment System and Multinational Enterprises*. Oxford: Oxford University Press.

Brittan, S. (2004) 'The Dollar Needs Benign Neglect', *Financial Times*, 30 January.

Bryman, A. and R. Burgess (eds) (1994) *Analyzing Qualitative Data*. London: Routledge.

Buckley, P. and M. Casson (1976) *The Future of the Multinational Enterprise*. London: Macmillan.

Buckley, P. and M. Casson (1998) 'Models of the Multinational Enterprise', *Journal of International Business Studies*, 29(1): 21–44.

Burt, T. (2001) 'General Motors in Brazil', *Financial Times*, 10 April.

Butler, K. (2006). 'Finance and the Search for the "Big" Question in International Business', *AIB Insights*. 3rd edition.

Casson, M. (2000) *Economics of International Business*. Cheltenham: Edward Elgar.

Caves, R. (1971) 'International Corporations: the Industrial Economics of Foreign Investment', *Economica*, 38.

Caves, R. (1974) 'Industrial Organization', in J. Dunning (ed.), *Economic Analysis and the Multinational Enterprise*. London: Allen & Unwin.

Chen, H. and T. Chen, T. (1998) 'Network Linkages and Location Choice in Foreign Direct Investment', *Journal of International Business Studies*, 29(3): 445–67.

Child, J. and Y. Lu (1996) 'Institutional Constraints on Economic Reform: the Case of Investment Decisions in China', *Organization Science* 7: 60–7.

Choi, C. and J. Kim (2003) 'The Asian Exposure of US Firms: Operational and Risk Management Strategies', *Pacific-Basin Finance Journal* 11: 121–38.

Choi, C., S. Lee and J. Kim (1999) 'A Note on Countertrade: Contractual Uncertainty and Transaction Governance in Emerging Economies', *Journal of International Business Studies*, 30: 189–201.

Choi, J. and A. Prasad (1995) 'Exchange Risk Sensitivity and its Determinants: a Firm and Industry Analysis', *Financial Management*, 24: 77–88.

Chow, E. and H. Chen (1998) 'The Determinants of Foreign Exchange Rate Exposure: Evidence on Japanese Firms', *Pacific-Basin Finance Journal*, 6: 153–74.

Chow, E., W. Lee and M. Solt (1997a) 'The Economic Exposure of US Multinational Firms', *Journal of Financial Research*, 20: 191–210.

Chow, E., W. Lee and M. Solt (1997b) 'The Exchange-rate Risk Exposure of Asset Returns', *Journal of Business*, 70: 105–23.

Clague, C. (1997) *Institutions and Economic Development: Growth and Governance in Less-developed and Post-socialist Countries*. Baltimore: Johns Hopkins University Press.

Cohen, M.A. and H. Lee (1989) 'Resource Deployment Analysis of Global Manufacturing and Distribution Networks', *Journal of Manufacturing and Operations Management* 2: 81–104.

Cramer, D. (2004) *Advanced Quantitative Data Analysis*. Maidenhead: Open University Press.

Creswell, J. (2003) *Research Design: Qualitative, Quantitative, and Mixed Methods Approaches*. London: Sage.

Creswell, J., V. Plano Clark, M. Gutmann and W. Hanson (2003) 'Advances in Mixed Method Design', in A. Tashakkori and C. Teddlie (eds), *Handbook of Mixed Methods in the Social and Behavioural Sciences*. Thousand Oaks, CA: Sage.

Czinkota, M., I. Ronkianen and M. Moffet (1996) *International Business*. Fort Worth, TX: The Dryden Press.

De Jong, A., J. Ligterink and V. Macrae (2002) 'A Firm-specific Analysis of the Exchange-rate Exposure of Dutch Firms', *ERIM Report Series Research in Management,* November.

Del Sol, P. and J. Kogan (2007) 'Regional Competitive Advantage Based on Pioneering Economic Reforms: The Case of Chilean FDI', *Journal of International Business Studies*, 38(6): 901–27.

Devlin, R., R. Grafton and D. Rowlands (1998) 'Rights and Wrongs: a Property Rights Perspective of Russia's Market Reforms', *Antritust Bulletin* 43: 275–96.

Dey, I. (1993) *Qualitative Data Analysis: a User-friendly Guide for Social Scientists*. London: Routledge.

DiMaggio, P. and W. Powell (1983) 'The Iron Cage Revisited: Institutional Isomorphism and Collective Rationality in Organizational Fields', *American Sociological Review*, 48: 147–60.

Doherty, N.A. and C.W.J. Smith (2001) 'Corporate Insurance Strategy: the Case of British Petroleum', in D.H.J. Chew (ed.), *The New Corporate Finance*. New York: McGraw-Hill.

Dominguez, K. and L. Tesar (2001) 'Exchage Rate Exposure', *NBER Working Paper,* Series 8453.

Donnelly, R. and E. Sheehy (1996) 'The Share Price Reaction of UK Exporters to Exchange Rate Movements: an Empirical Study', *Journal of International Business Studies*, 27: 157–65.

Doukas, J., P. Hall and L. Lang (2001) 'Exchange Rate Exposure at the Firm and Industry Level', *Financial Markets, Institutions, and Instruments,* 12: 291–346.

Doz, Y., S.J. Asa Kawa and P. Williamson (1997) 'The Metanational Corporation', *INSEAD Working Paper*.

Dunning, J. (1977) 'Trade, Location of Economic Activity, and the MNE: a Search for an Eclectic Approach', in B. Ohlin et al. (eds), *The International Allocation of Economic Activity*. London: Macmillan.

Dunning, J. (1995) 'Reappraising the Eclectic Paradigm in the Age of Alliance Capitalism', *Journal of International Business Studies*, 26(3): 461–91.

Dunning, J. (1996) 'The Geographical Sources of Competitiveness of Firms: the Results of a New Survey', *Transnational Corporations*, 5(3): 1–29.

Dunning, J. (2001a) 'The Eclectic (OLI) Paradigm of International Production: Past, Present, and Future', *Journal of the Economics of Business*, 8(2): 173–90.

Dunning, J. (2001b) *Oxford Handbook of International Business*. Oxford: Oxford University Press.

Dunning, J. (2003) 'Some Antecedents of Internalization Theory', *Journal of International Business Studies*, 34(2): 108–15.

Dunning, J. and S. Lundan (1998) 'The Geographical Sources of Competitiveness', *International Business Review*, 7(2): 115–33.

Easterby-Smith, M., R. Thorpe and A. Lowe (2002) *Management Research: an Introduction*. London: Sage.

ECLAC (2006a) *Foreign Investment in Latin America and the Caribbean*. Santiago de Chile: Economic Commission for Latin America and the Caribbean.

ECLAC (2006b) *Latin America and the Caribbean in the World Economy, 2005–2006*. Santiago de Chile: Economic Commission for Latin America and the Caribbean.

Enright, M. (1998) 'Regional Clusters and Firm Strategy', in A. Chandler et al. (eds), *The Dynamic Firm*. Oxford: Oxford University Press.

Enright, M. (2000) 'The Globalization of Competition and the Localization of Competitive Advantages: Policies Towards Regional Clustering', in N. Hood and S. Young (eds), *The Globalization of Multinational Enterprise Activity*. Basingstoke: Macmillan.

Estrin, S. and M. Wright (1999) 'Enterprise Performance and Corporate Governance in Ukraine', *Journal of Comparative Economics*, 27: 398–421.

European Bank for Reconstruction and Development (1998) *Transition Report 1998*. London: EBRD.

European Commission (2004) Retrieved from http://europa.eu.int/comm/external_relations/mercosur/bacground_doc/ on September 2004.

Faff, R. and A. Marshall (2005) 'International Evidence on the Determinants of Foreign Exchange Rate Exposure of Multinational Corporations', *Journal of International Business Studies*, 36(5): 539–58.

Fernandez-Arias, E. and R. Hausmann (2000) *Is FDI a Safer Form of Financing?* Washington, DC: Inter-American Development Bank.

Financial Times (1996) 'Japanese Industry: Learning to Live with a Strong Yen', *Financial Times*, 12 November.

Florida, R. (1995) 'Towards the Learning Region', *Futures*, 27.

Fornes, G. and G. Cardoza, G. (2005) 'Spanish Companies in Latin America: a Winding Road'. Paper presented at European International Business Academy, Oslo.

Fornes, G. and G. Cardoza (2006) 'Spanish Companies in Latin America: a Winding Road', *University of Bath School of Management Working Paper Series*, 2006 (08).

Fornes, G. and G. Cardoza (2008) 'Foreign Exchange Exposure in Emerging Markets. a Study of Spanish Companies in Latin America', *International Journal of Emerging Markets*, 4(1).

George, A. and C. Schroth (1991) 'Managing Foreign Exchange for Competitive Advantage', *Sloan Management Review*, 32: 105–16.

Gill, J. and P. Johnson (1997) *Research Methods for Managers*. London: Paul Chapman.

Glaser, B. and A. Strauss (1967) *The Discovery of Grounded Theory: Strategies for Qualitative Research*. New York: Aldine.

Guay, W. (1999) 'The Impact of Derivatives on Firm Risk: an Empirical Examination of New Derivative Users', *Journal of Accounting and Economics*, 26: 319–51.

Guillén, M.F. (2000) 'Business Groups in Emerging Economies: A Resource-Based View', *Academy of Management Journal*, 43(3): 362.

Gummesson, E. (2006) 'Qualitative Research in Management: Addressing Complexity, Context, and Persona', *Management Decision*, 44(2): 167–79.

Hagelin, N. and B. Pramborg (2004) 'Hedging Foreign Exchange Exposure: Risk Reduction from Transaction and Translation Hedging', *Journal of International Financial Management and Accounting*, 15(1): 1–20 .

Hakkarainen, A., N. Joseph, E. Kasanen and V. Puttonen (1998) 'The Foreign Exchange Exposure Management Practices of Finnish Industrial Firms', *Journal of International Financial Management and Accounting*, 9(1): 34–57.

Hardy, M. (1993) 'Regression with Dummy Variables', in M. Lewis-Beck (ed.), *Regression Analysis*. London: Sage.

Harris, J., J. Hunter and C. Lewis (1995) *The New Institutional and Third World Development*. London: Routledge.

He, J. and L. Ng (1998) 'The Foreign Exchange Exposure of Japanese Multinational Corporations', *Journal of Finance*, 53: 733–53.

Ho Park, S., S. Li and D. Tse (2006) 'Market Liberalization and Firm Performance During China's Economic Transition', *Journal of International Business Studies*, 37(1): 127–47.

Hodder, J. (1982) 'Exposure to Exchange-rate Movements', *Journal of International Economics* 13: 375–86.

Hoskisson, R.E., L. Eden, C.M. Lau and M. Wright (2000) 'Strategy in Emerging Economies', *Academy of Management Journal*, 43(3): 249.

Huchzermeier, A. (1993) *Global Supply Chain Competition*. Chicago: University of Chicago Press.

Huchzermeier, A. and M.A. Cohen (1996) 'Valuing Operational Flexibility Under Exchange Rate Risk', *Operations Research*, 44(1): 100.

Hussey, J. and R. Hussey (1997) *Business Research: a Practical Guide for Undergraduate and Postgraduate Students*. Basingstoke: Macmillan Business.

Hymer, S. (1960) *The International Operations of National Firms: a Study of Foreign Direct Investment*. Cambridge, MA: MIT Press.

Hymer, S. (1968) 'La grande "corporation" multinationale: Analyse de certaines raisons qui poussant à l'intégration internationale des affaires', *Revuu Economique*, 14(6): 949–73.

IADB (2006) *Inclusive Integration for Global Competitiveness: Strengthening the EU–LAC Partnership*. Washington, DC: Inter-American Development Bank.

Ietto-Gillies, G. (2000) 'What Role for Multinationals in the New Theories of International Trade and Location?', *International Review of Applied Economics*, 14(4): 413–26.

Jacque, L. (1981) 'Management of Foreign Exchange Risk: a Review Article', *Journal of International Business Studies* 12: 81–101.

Jefferson, G. and T. Rawski (1995) 'How Industrial Reform Worked in China: the Role of Innovation, Competition, and Property Rights', in M. Bruno and B. Pleskovic (eds), *Proceedings of the World Bank Annual Conference on Development Economics*. Washington DC: World Bank.

Jorion, P. (1990) 'The Exchange-rate Exposure of US Multinationals', *Journal of Business*, 63: 331–45.

Joseph, N. and R. Hewins (1997) 'The Motives for Corporate Hedging Among UK Multinationals', *International Journal of Finance & Economics*, 2: 151–71.

Kennedy, J. (1984) 'Risk Assessment for US Affiliates Based in Less Developed Countries', *Columbia Journal of World Business*, Summer: 76–9.

Kennedy, R.E. (2002) 'Project Valuation in Emerging Markets', *Harvard Business School Cases*.

Khanna, T. and K. Palepu (1997) 'Why Focused Strategies May be Wrong for Emerging Markets', *Harvard Business Review*, 4: 3–10.

Khanna, T. and K. Palepu (2000) 'The Future of Business Groups in Emerging Markets: Long-run Evidence from Chile', *Academy of Management Journal*, 43(3): 268.

Khanna, T. and K. Palepu (2002) 'Emerging Giants: Building World-Class Companies in Emerging Markets', *Harvard Business School Cases*.

Kobrin, S. (1977) *Foreign Direct Investment, Industrialization and Social Change*. Greenwich, CT: JAI Press.

Kogut, B. and Kulatilaka, N. (1994) 'Operational Flexibility, Global Manufacturing, and the Option Value of a Multinational Network', *Management Science*, 40(1): 123–39.

Kogut, B. and I. Zander (1994) 'Knowledge of the Firm and the Evolutionary Theory of the Multinational Corporation', *Journal of International Business Studies*, 24(4).

Kojima, K. (1982) 'Macro Economic Versus International Business Approaches to Foreign Direct Investments', *Hotosubashi Journal of Economics*, 23: 630–40.

Kubes, J. and G. Rädler (2003) 'Globalizing Volkswagen: Creating Excellence on All Fronts', *IMD Note 141, International Institute for Management Development*.

Kuemmerle, W. (1999) 'The Drivers of Foreign Direct Investment Into Research and Development: an Empirical Investment', *Journal of International Business Studies*, 30(1): 1–24.

La Porta, R., F. Lopez de Silanes, A. Shleifer and R. Vishny (1997) 'Legal Determinants of External Finance', *Journal of Finance* 52: 1131–50.

Lamming, R. (1993) *Beyond Partnership. Strategies for Innovation and Lean Supply*. Hemel Hempstead: Prentice Hall.

Lau, C. (1998). 'Strategic Orientations of Chief Executives in State-owned Enterprises in Transition', in M. Hitt et al. (eds), *Managing Strategically in an Interconnected World*. Chichester, UK: Wiley.

Lau, L. and J. Stiglitz (2005) 'China's Alternative to Revaluation', *Financial Times*, 24 April.

Lee, J. and D. Miller (1996) 'Strategy, Environment, and Performance in Two Technological Contexts: Contingency Theory in Korean Firms', *Organization Studies* 17: 729–50.

Lees, F. and L. Mauer (2002) 'American Companies Should Prepare for the UK Entering the Euro System', *Review of Business*, Fall.

Leontief, W. (1954) 'Domestic Production and Foreign Trade: the American Capital Position Re-examined', *Economia Internazionale*, 9(32).

Lessard, D. and J. Lightstone (1986) 'Volatile Exchange Rates Can Put Operations at Risk', *Harvard Business Review* 64: 61–76.

Levitt, T. (1983) 'The Globalization of Markets', *Harvard Business Review*, 61(3): 92.

Lewis-Beck, M. (ed.) (1993) *Regression Analysis*. London: Sage Publications.

Lowengart, O. and S. Mizrahi (2000) 'Applying International Reference Price: Market Structure, Information Seeking and Consumer Welfare', *International Marketing Review*, 17(6): 525.

Madura, J. (1995) *International Financial Management*. St Paul, MN: West Publishing Company.

Madura, J. and A. Tucker (1991) 'Impact of the Louvre Accord on Actual and Anticipated Exchange Rate Volatilities', *Journal of International Financial Markets, Institutions, and Money*, 1(2): 43–59.

Malmberg, A., O. Solvell and I. Zander (1996) 'Spatial Clustering, Local Accumulation of Knowledge and Firm Competitiveness', *Geographical Annals*, 78(2): 85–97.

Marshall, A. (2000) 'Foreign Exchange Risk Management in UK, USA, and Asia Pacific Multinational Companies', *Journal of Multinational Financial Management*, 2(10): 185–211.

Marshall, A. and P. Weetman (2002) 'Information Asymmetry in Disclosure of Foreign Exchange Risk Management: Can Regulation be Effective?', *Journal of Economic and Business*, 54: 31–53.

Marston, R. (2001) 'The Effects of Industry Structure on Economic Exposure', *Journal of International Money and Finance*, 20: 149–64.

Martin, A., J. Madura and A. Akhigbe (1999) 'Economic Exchange Rate Exposure of U.S.-based MNCs Operating in Europe', *Financial Review*, 34: 21–36.

Martin, A. and L. Mauer (2003) 'Transaction Versus Economic Exposure: Which Has Greater Cash Flow Consequences?', *International Review of Economics and Finance*, 12: 437–49.

McDonald, F. and Burton, F. (2002) *International Business*. London: Thomson.

McManus, J. (1972) 'The Theory of the International Firm', in G. Paquet (ed.), *The Multinational Firm and the Nation State*. Toronto: Collins and Macmillan.
Merrian, S. (1998) *Qualitative Research and Case Study Applications in Education*. San Francisco: Jossey-Bass.
Miles, I. and A. Huberman (1984) *Qualitative Data Analysis*. London: Sage.
Miller, K. and J. Reuer (1998) 'Firm Strategy and Economic Exposure to Foreign Exchange Rate Movements', *Journal of International Business Studies*, 29(3).
Mitchell, W.C. (1967) *Types of Economic Theory from Mercantilism to Institutionalism*. New York: Kelley.
Moon, H. (1999) *An Unconventional Theory of Foreign Direct Investment*. Seoul: Seoul National University.
Narayandas, D., J. Quelch and G. Swartz, G. (2000) 'Prepare Your Company for Global Pricing', *Sloan Management Review*, 42(1): 61.
Neary, P. (2003) 'Globalisation and Market Structure', *Journal of the European Economic Association*, 1(2–3): 245–71.
Nelson, J., C. Tilley and L. Walker (eds) (1998) *Transforming post-Communist Political Economies: Task Force on Economies in Transition, National Research Council*. Washington DC: National Academy Press.
Nguyen, H. and R. Faff (2003) 'Can the Use of Foreign Currency Derivatives Explain Variations in Foreign Exchange Exposure? Evidence from Australian Companies', *Journal of Multinational Financial Management*, 13: 193–215.
North, D. (1990) *Institutions, Institutional Change, and Economic Performance*. New York: Cambridge University Press.
Norton, E. and J. Malindretos (1991) 'FAS #52 and Exchange Rate Exposure: Hedging Strategies', *American Business Review*, June.
Ohlin, B. (1933) *Interregional and International Trade*. Cambridge MA: Harvard University Press.
Oliver, C. (1997) 'Sustainable Competitive Advantage: Combining Institutional and Resource-based Views', *Strategic Management Journal* 18: 697–713.
Oxelheim, L. (1984) *Foreign Exchange Risk Management in the Modern Company: A Total Perspective*. Stockholm: Scandinavian Institute for Foreign Exchange Research.
Palmer, D., P. Jennings and X. Zhou (1993) 'Late Adoption of the Multidivisional Form by US Corporations: Institutional, Political, and Economic Accounts', *Administrative Science Quarterly* 38: 100–31.
Pantzalis, C., B. Simkins and P. Laux (2001) 'Operational Hedges and the Foreign Exchange Exposure of US Multinational Corporations', *Journal of International Business Studies*, 32: 793–812.
Peng, M. (1997) 'Firm Growth in Transitional Economies: Three Longitudinal Cases from China, 1989–96', *Organization Studies*, 18: 385–413.
Peng, M. and P. Heath (1996) 'The Growth of the Firm in Planned Economies in Transition: Institutions, Organisations, and Strategic Choice', *Academy of Management Review* (21): 492–528.
Penrose, E. (1959) *The Theory of the Growth of the Firm*. White Plains, NY: Sharpe.

Pole, C. and R. Lampard (2002) *Practical Social Investigation: Qualitative and Quantitative Methods in Social Research*. Harlow: Pearson Education.

Porter, M. (1990) *The Competitive Advantage of Nations*. New York: Free Press.

Prahalad, C.K. and K. Lieberthal (2003) 'The End of Corporate Imperialism', *Harvard Business Review*, 81(8): 109.

Pringle, J. (1991) 'Managing Foreign Exchange Exposure', *Journal of Applied Corporate Finance*, 3: 73–82.

Pringle, J. (1995) 'A Look at Indirect Foreign Currency Exposure', *Journal of Applied Corporate Finance*: 8: 75–81.

Pringle, J. and R. Connolly (1993) 'The Nature and Causes of Foreign Currency Exposure', *Journal of Applied Corporate Finance*, 6: 61–72.

Quelch, J. (2003) 'The Return of the Global Brand', *Harvard Business Review*, 81(8): 22.

Ricardo, D. (2002) *The Principles of Political Economy and Taxation*. London: Empiricus Books.

Robson, C. (2002) *Real World Research: a Resource for Social Scientists and Practitioner-Researchers*. Oxford: Blackwell.

Rondinelli, D. (1998) 'Institutions and Market Development: Capacity Building for Economic and Social Transition', *IPPRED working paper no 14, Enterprise and Cooperative Development Department, International Labor Organization*.

Roulstone, D. (1999) 'Effect of SEC Financial Reporting Release no. 48 on Derivative and Market Risk Disclosures', *Accounting Horizons*, 13: 343–63.

Rugman, A., S. Collinson and R. Hodgetts (2006) *International Business*. Harlow: Pearson.

Rugman, A. and R. Hodgetts (2003) *International Business*. Harlow: Prentice Hall.

Saunders, M., P. Lewis and A. Thornhill (2003) *Research Methods for Business Students*. Harlow: FT Prentice Hall.

Schroeder, L., D. Sjoquist and P. Stephan (1986) *Understanding Regression Analysis: an Introductory Guide*. Beverly Hills: Sage.

Scott, W. (1995) *Institutions and Organizations*. Thousand Oaks, CA: Sage.

Shapiro, A. (1975) 'Exchange Rate Changes, Inflation, and the Value of the Multinational Corporation', *Journal of Finance*, 30: 485–502.

Shapiro, A. (1977) 'Developing a Profitable Exposure Management System', *Business International Money Report*, London: Economist Intelligence Unit.

Shapiro, A. (2003) *Multinational Financial Management*. New York: Wiley.

Shapiro, A. and Rutenberg, D. (1974) 'When to Hedge Against Devaluation', *Management Science*, 20(12): 1514–30.

Shin, H. and L. Soenen (1999) 'Exposure to Currency Risk by US Multinational Corporations', *Journal of Multinational Financial Management*, 9: 195–207.

Smith, A. and K. Sutherland (1993) *An Inquiry into the Nature and Causes of the Wealth of Nations: a Selected Edition*. Oxford: Oxford University Press.

Solvell, O. and J. Birkinshaw (2000) 'Multinational Enterprises and the Knowledge Economy: Leveraging Global Practices', in J. Dunning (ed.), *Regions,*

Globalisation, and the Knowledge Based Economy. Oxford: Oxford University Press.

Soulsby, A. and E. Clark, E. (1996) 'The Emergence of Post-communist Management in the Czech Republic', *Organization Studies*, 20: 227–47.

Storper, M. and H. Scott (1995) 'The Wealth of Regions', *Futures*, 27(5): 505–25.

Suarez, F. and R. Oliva (2002) 'Learning to Compete: Transforming Firms in the Face of Radical Environment Change', *Business Strategy Review*, 13: 62.

Suhomlinova, O. (1999) 'Constructive Destruction: Transformation of Russian State-owned Construction Enterprises During Market Transition', *Organization Studies*, 20: 451–84.

Sundaram, A. and S. Black (1992) 'The Environment and Internal Organization of Multinational Enterprises', *Academy of Management Review*, 17: 729–57.

Sundaram, A. and V. Mishra (1991) 'Currency Movements and Corporate Pricing Strategy', in S. Khoury (ed.), *Recent Developments in International Banking*. Amsetrdam: Elsevier Science Publishers.

Tashakkori, A. and C. Teddlie (1998) *Mixed Methodology: Combining Qualitative and Quantitative Approaches*. Thousand Oaks, CA: Sage.

Titscher, S., M. Meyer, R. Wodak and E. Vetter (2000) *Methods of Text and Discourse Analysis*. Thousand Oaks, CA: Sage.

UNCTAD (2002) 'Trends in International Production (Extract from World Investment Report, 2002)', *Economic Review*, 33(12): 5.

UNCTAD (2007) *World Investment Report*. Geneva: United Nations.

Vernon, R. (1966) 'International Investment and International Trade in the Product Cycle', *Quarterly Journal of Economics*, 80(2): 190.

Vernon, R. (1974) 'The Location of Economic Activity', in J. Dunning (ed.), *Economic Analysis and the Multinational Enterprise*. London: Allen & Unwin.

von Ungerm-Sternberg, T. and C. von Weizssacker, C. (1990) 'Strategic Foreign Exchange Management', *Journal of Industrial Economics*, 38: 381–95.

Wesson, T. (1993) *An Alternative Motivation for Foreign Direct Investment*. Cambridge, MA: Harvard University Press.

Wesson, T. (1997) 'A Model of Asset-Seeking Foreign Direct Investment'. Paper presented at The Administration Science Association of Canada.

White, H. (1980) 'A Heteroskedasticity-constant Covariance Matrix Estimator and a Direct Test for Heteroskedasticity', *Econometrica*, 48: 817–38.

Williamson, O. (1975) *Markets and Hierarchies Analysis and Antitrust Implications*. New York: Free Press.

World Bank (1996) *World Development Report*. Washington, DC: World Bank.

WTO (2003) *World Trade Organization Annual Report*. Geneva: World Trade Organization.

WTO (2007) *International Trade Statistics*. Geneva: World Trade Organization.

Index